DICK F

MW00715523

Reflections on a Man in His Wilderness

Edited by Alan and Laurel Bennett

Copyright © 2016 by Alan and Laurel Bennett
All rights reserved. This book or any portion thereof
may not be reproduced or used in any manner whatsoever
without the express written permission of the publisher
except for the use of brief quotations in a book review.

Printed in the United States of America

First Printing 2016

Table of Contents

iv

Acknowledgements

This project would not have been possible without the help of our contributors who took the time to share their memories of Dick Proenneke. First and foremost we thank Glen Alsworth Sr., David Clum, Margaret (Sis) Clum, Randy Weisser, Dick Hackard, John Branson, Craig Coray, Stu Ramstad, Jerry and Norma Holt, Leon Alsworth III, Jill Acheson, Stu Coleman, Paul Haertel, Larry Van Slyke, Frank and Jeanne Moore, Geraldine Straty, Tom Betts, Mrs. Frank (Kathy) Betts, Andy Hutchison, Clair Roberts, Patty Brown, Chris Degernes, Bob Swerer Jr, Alison Woodings, Lee Fink, John Erickson, Jeanette Mills, Sandy Lang, Monroe Robinson and Jana Walker. We are grateful to others that shared memories that we were not able to include.

We thank Rick Phillips for the use of his photographs of Dick, including those that appear on the front and back covers; and to Jill Acheson, Jeanette Mills, Clair Roberts, Dick Schmitz and Randy Weisser for the use of photographs that appear elsewhere in the book. We thank Jerry and Norma Holt for sharing their letters from Dick.

A special thanks to Paul Haertel for providing contact information for a number of former National Park Service employees that we would have otherwise never tracked down. Jill Acheson and K. Schubeck and Monroe Robinson's enthusiastic encouragement fueled our motivation to complete this project.

Jeanette Mills also provided a steady stream of encouragement throughout this project and was helpful in crosschecking dates and facts about Dick's years at Twin Lakes. A special thanks to Lake Clark resident Anne Coray for having the interest and taking the time to edit a final draft of this book.

Finally, we wish to thank an anonymous donor in the State of Alaska for contributing proceeds from the Proenneke's estate toward publication of these precious memories of Dick.

Photo courtesy of Jeanette Mills

Introduction

In 1968, at the age of fifty-two, Richard (Dick) Proenneke constructed a log cabin on the edge of a remote wilderness lake in southwest Alaska and lived there alone for thirty years. His story became widely known in 1973 when Sam Keith published the book *One Man's Wilderness-an Alaskan Odyssey,* based on Proenneke's journals and photography. After years in print it was re-issued in a new format in 1999, winning that year's National Outdoor Book Award.

Dick's popularity grew after Bob Swerer Sr. and his son edited and added sound and narration to some of the over 3,000 feet of 8- and 16-mm movie film shot by Dick during his early years at Twin Lakes. Swearer Productions created a series of videos under the titles *Alaska Silence and Solitude, The Frozen North,* and *Alone in the Wilderness I and II.* In 2003, some of the copyrighted text from the book and the films began appearing nationally on U.S. Public Television.

But Dick Proenneke's story is far more than a man living in the wilderness. Despite the title given to his films, only in the dead of winter was he truly "alone" at Twin Lakes. His journals are filled with accounts of visits from hunters, fisherman, neighbors, friends and family, and deliveries of mail and supplies by three generations of the Alsworth family. Dick assisted others in recovering and salvaging downed aircraft, helped with searches and rescues, and participated in wildlife surveys. He hosted friends for extended stays at his cabin, interacted with National Park Service planning teams and film crews, reported hunting violations, greeted visitors, lead hikes, assisted seasonal park rangers, and collected and maintained records on the weather and the annual cycles of plants and animals.

Dick frequently traveled to Lake Clark and Port Alsworth by air or on foot, where he visited friends, assisted in building log structures, repaired heavy equipment, graded aircraft runways, planted and harvested vegetables, and in later years house-sat during the winter months. For many years Dick made an annual sixty-mile round trip hike to the Bonanza Hills to assist his friends in the maintenance of a John Deere bulldozer.

Thousands have been inspired by Dick's lifestyle, craftsmanship, and wilderness skills, but few know much of the man himself. Park rangers and volunteers serving as interpretive guides at the Richard L. Proenneke National Historic Site today are often asked by visitors: "What was Dick really like when he was living here?" Many can answer that question. They are the bush pilots, fishing and hunting guides, local friends, and past and present National Park Service staff who knew and interacted with Dick over the thirty years that he lived at Twin Lakes.

Dick touched many lives and left long-lasting impressions. Those who knew Dick can vividly recall the first time they met him. They can also remember the hikes, canoe paddles, overnight stays in his cabin, and the weather—which often had the final say on what happened when they visited him. Many experienced the aroma and taste of Dick's beans, fried lake trout, fireweed salad, sourdough hotcakes, and biscuits. Others followed Dick to his favorite blueberry picking spot, carrying one of the tin buckets that he crafted from a discarded fuel can. Dick's inquisitive nature fascinated everyone. There was Dick's letter writing, his mail, and the various ways that his mail carriers delivered it. Many admired his yearly wall calendars filled with daily weather records, first sightings of robins in spring, and the last day of the year on which the sun would strike his cabin. There were times when others needed Dick's help, and there were times when Dick needed the help of others.

We owe a debt of gratitude to him for recording so much with pen and camera, because there may never be another Dick Proenneke or another wilderness like the one he experienced. His journals and films have allowed us to paddle up and down the lakes with him, share what he felt the first time he climbed to the top of Crag Mountain, and follow his day-by-day routine over the seasons and years.

As a tribute to Dick on the one hundredth anniversary of his birth, we invited those who knew him to characterize the kind of person he was, and to recall their memories, experiences, and stories. Most reflections of Dick are oral accounts given extemporaneously and later turned into a compilation of separate written tributes. Some chose to place their memories on paper with pen and ink, in a tradition true to

Dick. The contributors have many different perspectives and speak to Dick's resourcefulness, craftsmanship, passion for filming wildlife, physical and mental toughness, humor, and compassion.

Our contributors shine a light on aspects of Dick's everyday life. How did Dick add narration to the film *The Frozen North* without looking at the scenes? What started Dick's tradition of having visitors to his cabin sign a guest book—a tradition that continues today? How many miles did Dick put on the pedometer during the first two months after he received it from his brother Raymond? How many times did Dick say to the pilot, "*The ice is fine*" but then it wasn't? What did he do with all those small ketchup packets visitors left behind after eating lunch on his beach? What in the world are oat groats, and why did Dick switch to eating them instead of oatmeal? Is there any rhyme or reason behind all those little circles, arrows, and sketches on Dick's wall calendars? Why were the women that gave Dick advice on cooking, housekeeping, or his diet rarely invited back to his cabin? And what was that password that hikers needed to give the Sentinel before he allowed them to enter Low Pass?

The letters? Many people, long after they stopped traveling to visit Dick at Twin Lakes, stayed connected to him through letter writing. No tribute to Dick would be complete without acknowledging how his letters provided others a window into his daily life and the seasonal drama of nature he witnessed at Twin Lakes. Some of Dick's longest running correspondents were his friends from Kodiak Island. Like many, they treasured and retained most of their letters from Twin Lakes. Our tribute to Dick concludes with a sampling of his letters.

Hey, we're going to get that thing right out of there

Glen Alsworth Sr.

June 22, 1968. Got up before the sun and watched it light the tops of the mountains. The sound of a plane. In came Babe landing downwind. I saw his boy Glen climb out of the pilots side. That little fellow in the 8ᵗʰ grade next year was flying the old T-craft! RLP

The wind was blowing from the east as I descended and landed my ski-equipped Taylorcraft on the ice in front of Jay and Bella Hammond's home on the north shore of Lake Clark. I had flown over with a friend who wanted to meet the Hammond's caretaker, Dick Proenneke. We were delivering Dick's mail and some supplies that he had requested.

When I landed I stayed near shore because there wasn't any way to tell how thick the ice was. As the airplane came to a stop it weather-cocked into the wind. This meant that my skis were now perpendicular to the beach, and the plane could start sliding. At Lake Clark the ice freezes along the shoreline first, then as the water level drops, the ice sinks and creates a shelf that slopes lakeward. Sure enough, when I pulled in to stop and shut down, the airplane started sliding out further from shore. When it was fifteen or twenty feet from the shoreline the plane broke through the ice. The water wasn't too deep, only about four or five feet at the nose of the plane. The tail remained on top of the ice. I got out easily and didn't even get my feet wet, but we were stranded.

By this time Dick had walked out from the Hammonds' house and was standing at the shoreline. His first words were: "Hell, we're going to get that thing right out of there."

When it came to recovering aircraft, Dick was right in his element. He instantly masterminded a plan. First, he ran back to the woodshed and grabbed some chainsaws; we used the saws to cut the ice behind the plane and push some of the chunks under the existing ice. That did two things: it got the ice out of the way plus it doubled the thickness where we had to stand to work beside the plane. Second, we tied a big come-along up to a tree and used it to pull the plane back onto safe ice and up to the beach where we could tie it down. We had the plane high and dry in forty minutes, and soon we went to work removing the magnetos [small electrical generators that produce voltage to fire the aircraft spark plugs]. We took the magnetos up to the wood stove and set them on the oven door to dry them out.

Dick had access to all sorts of tools there at the Hammond's and he seemed to know where they were and how to use them. I don't know if he had really worked on airplanes to speak of, but he knew all about magnetos. While the magnetos were drying we returned to the airplane, drained the oil out of the crankcase, and let it sit until the oil and water separated. Then we poured the water off.

The last issue we had to deal with was the electrical wiring harnesses that run from the magnetos to the spark plugs. They'd gotten wet, but we didn't have a way to take them up to the house and dry them out. The next morning the engine fired up but it had an intermittent miss from moisture in one of those wires. We still managed to fly it back home.

* * *

My first memory of Dick is from 1967. He'd never been to Port Alsworth, but he'd arranged to have my Dad (Babe) fly him to Upper Twin Lake where he would cut the logs to build his cabin. He seemed exceptionally energetic, and he didn't arrive with all the usual camping gear that tourists, fisherman, and hunters haul along with them today. His gear was less than fancy, and I sort of wondered how he was going to survive out there. My Dad liked Dick from the moment he arrived. I think what impressed my Dad most was Dick's willingness to work. Dick never sat around; he was always doing something, putting all his energy into it, and completing whatever he started. He had that good old fashioned Mid-western work ethic and my Dad respected that immensely.

The weather was not good on the morning they planned to fly up to Twin Lakes so Dick had to wait around until late that afternoon. In this situation, most of the people my Dad flew out to bush camps would have been pestering and asking, "Hey, do you think we can go yet?" or "How's the weather looking now?" Not Dick though; he left that judgement to the pilot. Instead, he asked if he could help prepare the potato garden or cut some firewood.

It was lucky for me that Dick arrived right about the time my Dad was teaching me how to fly. Taking Dick to and from Twin Lakes and hauling him supplies provided the perfect opportunity for me to get flying time. I never had any formal flight training, so a trip to Dick's was a handy excuse for me to get a lesson and gain experience.

I didn't realize it at the time, but earning Dick's respect and friendship would pay off in future years. After my parents moved away from Port Alsworth, our D-4 Caterpillar broke down and I had no idea what to do with it. I flew up to talk to Dick and asked if he might be able to come down and help me get it going. Dick couldn't get away immediately, but a few days later I flew back to get him.

As soon as we touched down in Port Alsworth he grabbed a box full of wrenches from the hanger and tore into that D-4 Cat. We had no manual for it, no parts list, nothing. He went into that machine from the outside in, taking pieces and parts off here and there. After a short while he climbed out and said, "Well, I think we need to change out a piston in the number 4 cylinder, and replace a drive gear that is stripped out." Both jobs sounded intimidating and challenging to me because they meant working down in the bowels of the machine. But Dick just went right to it, never slowed up a minute. He went right down to the piston that we needed, he located the part number and got it ordered, and then he started on the drive system. He had to pull the track off and remove a sprocket. Those parts might have been on that shaft for half a century. Dick worked all day and tried almost every trick in his book but that sprocket would not come loose.

I said, "It's hopeless, that thing is never going to come off." Dick looked at me and said, "What? Somebody put it on there; it's got to come off."

Early the next day he put heat on the gear to make it expand. Then we took turns hitting it with a big sledge hammer to try to break it loose. It really hurts your arms when you hit steel like that because it vibrates and sends shock waves back all the way to your shoulders. But we took turns and kept hitting on it. It made a real crisp ring when we hit it, like a big church bell. As we were pounding away—and I can't remember if I was hitting it or Dick was hitting it—the tone abruptly changed. Instead of ringing, it just went thud when the hammer hit. Dick immediately stopped, laid down the hammer, turned off the heat and said, "Okay, it's off."

To me, it didn't look as if it had moved at all. But just from the sound of it Dick knew that it had broken loose. And sure enough, he took the nuts off and the sprocket just slid right off. Piece of cake. Then he went inside the drive train, inside the gear case and found the gear that was stripped out. We ordered all the parts. I took him back home for a few days till all the parts were gathered up and then brought him back down. In a few hours he had it going like new. It's still running!

* * *

One of the things that was fascinating about Dick was his insatiable curiosity. I remember when we got our first microwave. He was visiting us and he'd never seen a microwave before. So we showed him how it worked by heating up a cup of tea. Then we gave him a cup and told him to try it. Bewildered and puzzled, he walked around the microwave, opened and closed the door, put his cup inside and heated it for fifteen seconds. He took it out, tested the tea, and put the cup back in and heated it a little longer. Finally he looked at us and said, "How does that thing do this?" And for the rest of his visit he was like a little kid with a new toy, trying to figure out how in the world that magic box could make the food or water hot. But his curiosity didn't end there. After he went home and I visited him three weeks later, he started asking me questions about that microwave.

* * *

When they came out with satellite telephones they were big, pretty clumsy, and only worked intermittently. I tried one of them from different locations in the wilderness, and if you were persistent you could make it work. One day I mentioned it to Dick.

I said, "You ought to carry one of these satellite phones."

Dick replied, "What for?"

I said, "Well, if you're up on the mountain and you have an accident you could call out."

"What!" he said. "Have an accident; you don't have accidents at Twin Lakes."

I said, "But what if you're up there on a mountain and you have to cross a slide to get a good picture of the sheep? And the slide gives way and you go roaring down the mountain, get hurt, and can't walk back?"

"No!" he said. "You don't cross a slide."

I said, "Well, how do you get over there?"

Dick replied, "You walk back down to the lakeshore and you walk along and you go up the other mountain." He said, "You don't have accidents."

I said, "What if you paddle your canoe across the lake and get stranded over there?"

"Oh," he said, "It happens many times."

I said, "What do you do?"

He said, "You walk home, you don't take a chance; accidents don't happen to you. You cause them."

He had a pretty disciplined approach to hiking and being out in the wilderness. And it was no different when he was on a long distance hike. He was prepared, in good physical shape, and he carried food and emergency supplies. He didn't just strike out hiking somewhere without giving it a lot of thought and a lot of preparation. He didn't have fancy stuff but he took what he needed to make sure he survived and he didn't take any chances.

If Dick was gone when I landed at his cabin he would have a pin on a map with a note: "Gone here today." The pin would sometimes be twenty miles away! On those days I would just leave his mail and a note telling him I'd drop in again in a few days. If he had outgoing mail that was already sealed I could take it with me. But any letters that were still left open I of course had to leave behind.

There'd be days I'd land and see his note "Gone here today, should be back by eight or nine at night." If his destination was past the Lower Lake, then I'd fly down the shoreline on my way out in case he was coming back up the beach. And sometimes I'd find him hiking there; I'd pick him up and fly him home. Not because he wanted to ride home, but rather because I wanted to get the rest of his outgoing mail. On those days he would rattle up a little fire in the stove and reheat the beans and give me a bowlful.

Speaking of beans, he ate a lot of beans. Sourdoughs for breakfast, beans for dinner. He would just put a pot of beans on the stove and let it sit there and bubble away while he made biscuits. I hauled a lot of food up to him from our farm. It seemed like every time we went up, which was usually once or twice a month, we would take a couple dozen eggs. Dick would take about fifty pounds of potatoes up in the fall, and that would last him until February. Then we'd bring him another fifty pounds. He ate pretty simply, and, interestingly enough, we concluded that that was his preference. However, he did break his Twin Lakes tradition when he would come down for a few days to help us dig potatoes or fix equipment. He had a voracious appetite, and he would eat everything my wife Patty would fix: spaghetti, pizza or whatever she made. He loved it all.

Dick also loved his oatmeal. My Dad used to feed our goats barley and oats. Originally we tried to feed them some Quaker Oats, the same kind you would make cereal from. The goats would try to eat it, but each time they'd start sneezing. After a few days they wouldn't even touch it! We thought that it must have contained too much dust or chaff. So my Dad bought something from the feed store that was called oat groats, an animal food that came in fifty-pound sacks but hadn't been processed and refined like Quaker Oats. One morning we cooked some and discovered that oat groats retained their shape and didn't turn to mush like oatmeal. Dad liked them and so did the rest of the family. Well, it wasn't long before Dick found out about this and ordered a supply. Dick loved them, and thereafter oat groats was the only type of oats he would eat.

* * *

I think Dick's resourcefulness was the key to his ability to live alone all those years at Twin Lakes. One year I flew Dick and Will Troyer, a wildlife biologist working for the park, to Turquoise Lake to observe caribou calving. Turquoise Lake is on a subalpine plateau twenty miles north of Twin Lakes. I dropped them off there in the middle of May and a week later I picked them up and brought Will back to Port Alsworth. On the way back he told me about an incident that happened while they were camping.

One afternoon the inseam of Dick's pants tore from his foot clear up to his crotch. His pants were just flapping in the wind where the seam used to be. They were in the middle of a caribou calf count, the wind was getting stronger, and the noise of Dick's flapping trousers was getting louder. Finally, Will asked, "What are you going to do?"

Dick paused and replied, "Oh, I'm going to go visit a seamstress." He handed his clipboard to Will, turned toward the lake and took off. An hour passed and Will looked up to see Dick coming back with his pants neatly sewed up. Astonished, Will asked, "Well ... how did you do that?"

Dick explained that he'd gone down to the creeks at the head of Turquoise Lake. He knew that sport fisherman used that area during the summer and invariably somebody got a snag in their line so they would just cut the line off and throw it on the beach or in the bushes. He searched the area and soon found some monofilament fishing line and a discarded beer can. Next he used his knife to cut a narrow wedge-shaped piece of metal out of that beer can, and he rolled it up tight in the shape of a needle. Finally, he used his knife to drill a hole in the wider end of the needle. Then it was a simple matter of threading the needle with his monofilament line and getting on with the business of sewing his pants. Will was absolutely amazed.

* * *

A week or so before Dick's 80th birthday I flew up to deliver his mail. As I nosed the floats into his beach Dick came down and I asked if he had any plans for his birthday. He said, "I've been practicing chin ups so that on my birthday I can do eighty."

He was up to sixty when I landed, and he said he was adding two to four a day. Sadly, I missed his birthday, but I did get up to see him a week later. First thing I asked him was, "Did you do those eighty chin ups? "Oh, I felt good that morning," Dick said. "I got up, did those eighty chin ups." Then he paused. "I felt so good," he continued, "I just went ahead and did a hundred."

After sharpening his teenage flying skills delivering Dick Proenneke's mail, Glen Alsworth Sr. went on to become a legend in Alaskan aviation and a highly respected public servant as Mayor of the Lake and Peninsula Borough, a position he has held since 1989. Over the decades Glen has accumulated more than 35,000 flight hours, much of that flying in Alaska's challenging terrain and ever-changing weather conditions. He was the first American to fly, land, and overnight an American airplane in Pevek, Russia and has traveled to twenty-three other countries on six continents. When he is not flying passengers for Lake Clark Air, he volunteers his flying skills for Samaritan's Purse Humanitarian Aid Program, specializing in the Chukotka Russian Far East.

As a little kid, it seemed to me like Dick was part of our family

David Clum

August 12, 1972. Last night at twelve I was awakened by a racket out front. The miserable porcupine no doubt and if he climbed to the table with all the blueberries, I would be pretty unhappy. RLP

My first memories of Dick were when he would stay with us at our home in Anchorage. After arriving from Iowa in his Dodge pickup truck he'd spend a few days with us before heading out to his cabin at Twin Lakes. He would park his truck on our extra lot and that is where it would live for the summer. If he didn't come out in the fall to drive back to Iowa it just stayed parked on our lot year-round.

When he stayed with us he was always looking for something to do. I never saw him just sitting around. One year he built us a kennel for our dog. I still have a stool that he made for us. If something was broken Dick would fix it.

I visited Dick at his cabin for the first time in January when my dad was hauling supplies in for Dick. Unlike today, we used to have real winter back then. In January it would be thirty below zero or so at Port Alsworth, but when you got to Dick's place it would be at least forty below. That's what it was on that clear day when my dad and I landed on the lake. Dick had knocked down the big snowdrifts with his snowshoes but the landing was still sort of bumpy.

There was a lot of snow covering everything, including the trees. When I got out of the airplane every little sound was muffled. If I stopped walking and the snow wasn't crunching under my feet it was dead silent, hauntingly quiet. It was almost like time was standing still. Now and then the silence would be broken by a raven squawking in the distance.

As we walked toward the cabin I remember seeing Dick's watering hole that he had cut into the lake ice. That was something—it was just constantly, constantly freezing up and he had to keep chopping it open every day. He had a round block of wood pushed into the hole and then he mounded snow over the top. While I was huddled up next to his wood stove I kept thinking how hard the winter must be for Dick, by himself there with no communication. It was a constant battle to keep the drifts knocked down so airplanes could land, and every day he had to chop ice, shovel snow, carry water, and haul wood.

The following summer my grandfather (Babe Alsworth) dropped me off to stay with Dick for a few weeks. I had never been in a canoe before. The next day Dick put the canoe in the lake, handed me a paddle, and told me to get up front and paddle, end of instructions. Off we went; he steered and paddled from the back while I paddled in the front.

It was the same with hiking. "Let's go," said Dick, and off we went. I don't know how much he was slowing down for me or if he was at all, I couldn't tell. But we'd go hiking an awfully long distance. By six or seven in the evening when we were finally back at the cabin I'd usually be pretty well worn out and I'd sleep all night long. But I really enjoyed the hiking. We saw sheep, caribou, and other animals. We even hiked up to the glaciers at the far ends of the valleys.

In the evening I watched Dick writing in his journal. I remember him sitting down there for maybe an hour or more at a time. One night he said he wanted me to sit down and start a journal. Being a little kid I was not inclined to start writing a journal but Dick insisted. He never said why, and to this day I don't know whether it was for my sake or for my parents.

During my stay Dick carved me wooden spoons and then a little wooden boat while I watched. When I found a little piece of wood that looked like a pistol, Dick took it and did a little carving on it to make it look more authentic.

I remember Dick had trouble with porcupines while I was there. They kept chewing on the cabin and other wooden objects. One morning Dick pushed a porcupine into an old gas can with a shovel and then tamped the lid on. Earlier in the week I'd been looking around at all the stuff inside his cabin and I picked up a little ink jar that was filled with black sand. I said to Dick, "Boy, I'd sure like to have some of that black sand."

That morning with the porcupine Dick handed me some empty jars and said, "Let's go get some of that black sand and take the porcupine along."

Sure enough, at the head of the lake there was a lot of black sand; Dick called it magnetite. It was thick, with a lot of iron in it. I filled my ink bottles while Dick released the porcupine and then walked around to check out the animal tracks.

* * *

Dick was not a big storyteller with me. He was more interested in what was going on in my life or things that my family was doing. He was not much of a talker unless the subject turned to something that perked his interest, like airplanes. He was always curious and always wanted to learn. In later years when I visited him I was flying for Peninsula Airways. I piloted a couple of different airplanes that he was not familiar with. He asked a lot of questions about their engines, landing gear, navigation systems, and how they performed. He never forgot who I was. He'd recognize and greet me warmly even after he hadn't seen me for a couple of years.

* * *

Margaret (Sis) Clum

I will always remember Dick as a kind, quiet fellow, who parked his camper at our house, helped us with whatever needed to be done, and asked for little in return. We offered him space in the house, but most of the time he would stay in his camper. When we offered him our shower or bathtub he chose to take a sponge bath in the sink. That's how he lived, Twin Lakes or Anchorage.

He was very, very neat and he lived by the creed "you don't throw anything away." I had an old wicker hamper that my boys put their dirty clothes in. It had been used for many years and it was coming apart. One day at breakfast I finally said I was going to throw it out. "Oh no, I can fix that," said Dick. Just as quickly he took that hamper apart, down to the last nail and staple. He repaired and reassembled it and my son is still using it.

Dick was not one to ask for help if he felt that he could get by without it. One year he was in Anchorage and didn't tell us. Later we found out that he'd gone to Providence Hospital and had hernia surgery. After surgery he just stayed in his camper in the parking lot at the hospital! Anyone who has experienced post-surgery recovery can only grimace at the thought of doing that.

I visited Dick at his cabin a number of times. If I hadn't known it was Dick's cabin I could have guessed. Everything was neat, clean, and in order, even the woodpile. He didn't have a radio but I was always amazed at how he always seemed to know what was going on in the world. He picked up news by quizzing visitors and from magazines sent to him by his brother and sisters.

David Clum grew up spending summers at his parent's cabin at Tommy Creek along the shores of Lake Clark. He became a pilot like his grandfather, Babe Alsworth, and now flies as a Captain for Alaska Airlines.

Babe and Mary Alsworth's only daughter, Margaret Clum, opened her Anchorage home to family friend Dick Proenneke. Margaret can often be found running the front desk in the Lake Clark Air office at Merrill Field.

Dick seemed to know every big game animal in the area

Randy Weisser

"August 26. Early in the afternoon we heard a plane coming up the lake. A Super Widgeon (twin-engine floatplane) of Kodiak Airways. It was Dick Weisser and his son Randy coming to work on their cabin. We all worked to move their load of supplies to their cabin site and then cut and packed in some logs while they built their shelter". RLP

My Dad worked at the Navy base on Kodiak Island for thirty years or more. During those years he became close friends with Spike and Hope Carrithers, who lived just a few hundred yards from a cabin we owned forty miles outside the city of Kodiak. The tsunami generated during the 1964 Alaska Earthquake destroyed our cabin. After that Spike and Hope generously allowed us to stay with them while we were rebuilding. I believe Dick Proenneke stayed there also for a spell, possibly for a winter when the Carrithers were gone.

For a time my Dad hunted in the interior of Alaska near Trinity Lakes and Cold Creek Lake. After he became better acquainted with the Carrithers he began hunting in the Twin Lakes area where they had built a log cabin. Eventually Dad became interested in staking out a five-acre piece of land next to them on Upper Twin Lake and building his own cabin.

While I was in high school, it must have been 1965 or 1966, I flew up to Twin Lakes for the first time with my Dad. The Carrithers were there, and they let us stay in their guest cabin [Hope's Cabin] that Spike and Dick Proenneke had built a year or two earlier. My Dad and Spike cleared and leveled an area one hundred yards up the lake and began constructing our log cabin. By the end of our stay we were able to get all four walls erected, but we did not start on the roof. Dick Proenneke was not there at the time. Had he been there, I'm sure we would have made more progress than we did.

We returned the next summer to finish up. This time Dick and his brother Raymond were there. They were staying in Hope's Cabin so we stayed in a makeshift tent on this trip. We used some spruce poles to make a lean-to and covered it with rolled roofing. I remember one morning waking up to either camp robbers or magpies poking holes through the top of the "tent."

Work on the cabin went much quicker on this trip. Dick helped us cut the purlin and ridge logs. My Dad and I carried the small end of the logs and Dick carried the heavy end. He was in amazing shape. I also remember that when we were looking for the smaller trees (which were laid as rafter poles on the purlins) Dick went up the lake in his canoe with his brother to find the type of trees we needed. Dick knew where to look. He cut a bunch of poles for us and floated them down the lake. I was quite impressed with that.

Although I was too young to have much interaction with Dick at the time, I learned from my Dad that in addition to being a master carpenter, Dick was a great mechanic. I do remember from our visits with him at Twin Lakes that he was definitely a mountain man and in great shape. While we were there we saw the big stack of logs from the spruce that he had cut down and hauled to his cabin site. He was letting them dry for a year or so before he started building. He seemed to be able to invent whatever he needed, including a tool that he used to drag those heavy logs across the tundra to his building site near the lake.

In each of the trips I made with my Dad to Twin Lakes to build the cabin, we would set aside one day for hunting in order to take back meat for the family. On one occasion we saw a moose across the lake and Dick agreed to take us over there in his canoe to a strategic spot, in hopes that we would have a chance at taking some moose meat home. We hiked up the hill to our chosen vantage point but were never able to locate the moose. I remember my Dad saying later he suspected that after Dick had dropped us off he had gone down to where the moose was supposed to be to scare it off so it wouldn't be there when we came within range, which puzzled my Dad.

After recently reading Dick's journals, I think that could very likely have been the case. Dick seemed to know every big game animal in the area and he became quite protective, which I can fully understand. After failing to see the moose, my Dad and I hiked on down the lake because he wanted to take a look at an area where he and

Herb Wright used to hunt Dall sheep. After that we came down to the Lower Lake where we found a lone caribou. All that hiking paid off; we had our meat to take home after all. We left the caribou hanging in a tree beside the lake for fetching later. Then we hiked back up the lake to where Dick could see us and he paddled over to get us.

Our plan was to have the Widgeon from Kodiak Air, which was scheduled to pick us up the next day or two, land with us on the lower lake to load up the caribou. As it turned out, the pilot wasn't agreeable to that plan because of the weight load, so Spike told us he would make sure that it got brought back up to the cabin. I imagine he and Dick took the canoe down there and brought the caribou back up, then kept it under smoke for a couple of weeks. When Spike returned to Kodiak he brought it with him and gave it to my Dad. I remember my parents commenting that it was the best tasting caribou they had ever had, tender and smoky.

After we finished the cabin that fall we never went back to Twin Lakes, probably because when Spike, Hope, and my Dad staked out those lots and built the cabins, it was with the assumption that one day they could gain title to the land. I do know that when the National Park was created my Dad corresponded for some time with the Park Service about honoring the terms of the original lease, but eventually he realized that that wasn't going to happen. That was probably the main factor in not going back. But I think he probably also lost interest around that time in the big hunting expeditions that he and Herb Wright used to go on, as he never did make those kinds of trips again. I would love to return some time, and I think my sisters would also enjoy seeing the place they heard so much about.

Randy Weisser is among the few that spent time at Twin Lakes when Dick Proenneke was a "guest" of the Carrithers and not a resident in his own log cabin. The cabin that Spike, Dick, and his father built still stands. After becoming the property of Lake Clark National Park, Weissers cabin has filled a valuable role in maintaining the Proenneke National Historic Site. It also served as the on-site woodworking shop in which Monroe Robinson replicated many of Dick's original artifacts.

Do not take council of your fears

Dick Hackard

July 12, 1969. I heard a plane – the little black bird sure enough. A circle up country and in for a perfect landing. Babe with [my] nephew Dick Hackard. Good to have him at Twin Lakes. RLP

After I graduated from high school in 1969 I wrote my uncle, Dick Proenneke, in Alaska, asking him if I could come up for a visit and bring along a friend of mine. We spent months planning our trip to Twin Lakes and the time we would spend visiting Dick. But sadly when it got close to our departure date, my friend's Dad wouldn't let him go.

I was so excited about going to see my uncle that I went by myself. I drove to Peoria, Illinois and flew to Chicago where I went standby on a flight to Alaska. I didn't have a ticket so I just waited for an opening. Upon arriving in Anchorage Dick had arranged for me to stay with Margaret (Sis) Clum, Babe Alsworth's daughter. The following day I caught a commercial flight from Anchorage to Iliamna. From there one of Babe Alsworth's sons flew down to pick me up and take me to Port Alsworth. It was a long, exhausting trip and I spent most of the next day relaxing in Babe and Mary Alsworth's home.

Babe was the bush pilot that Dick relied on for his mail, supplies, and transportation to and from Twin Lakes. He was a very religious man and during my stay he played some of his taped sermons and told me about his missionary work in the nearby villages. That was fine with me because I was a Christian and I went to church regularly.

The next day the weather had cleared and he loaded me into his floatplane for the flight to Twin Lakes. I had never flown in a floatplane before and I really enjoyed that ride with Babe. It was a calm morning and he sat there in his pilot's seat looking so relaxed. I knew he'd made the flight hundreds and hundreds of times. At one point he'd have his chin resting on his hands and part of the time I swear he was asleep. He wasn't, of course, but he just seemed to be. He was so

- 16 -

used to flying that route up to Twin Lakes. In a letter Dick sent me before I left Iowa he said, "If the weather's bad Babe will wait it out, he won't take chances."

Upper Twin Lake was glassy calm when we landed in front of Dick's cabin in the Taylorcraft. Dick knew from my letters that I was coming and he was standing on the beach to meet us. His first words to me were, "Where's your buddy?" I replied, "Well, he had an accident in his Dad's car and as punishment he wasn't allowed to come, so I'm here alone."

Babe was in a hurry so we unloaded my gear and Dick's supplies. My eyes were drawn to the mountains as I walked back and forth between the beach and Dick's cabin. I felt like I was in another world. I was from the settled Midwest and not very prepared to step into Dick Proenneke's wilderness. Of course Dick sensed this immediately and made fun of me because I didn't have any hiking boots. In fact, I really didn't have any clothing fit for life at Twin Lakes. Fortunately it was early summer and the warmest time of the year. I did have rain gear, but Dick said he thought the first good wind would rip it to shreds.

The mountains were beautiful but looked intimidating. I didn't sleep too well my first night thinking about how I'd do hiking alongside Dick. I'd heard stories from my grandparents about Dick's long hikes through the mountains. I was a flat-lander, but worse yet one of my legs was shorter than the other and I had a slightly deformed foot. Dick understood my physical limitations and was very considerate. He took me on shorter hikes to begin with, then gradually added longer hikes to acclimate me. I can't remember having any real problems. He took me up Hope Creek canyon to a glacier. Of course that was just a warm up for Dick, he left me standing there while he took off and climbed a mountain peak overlooking the glacier. On later hikes we went to what he called "Gold Mountain" and followed a valley around its backside where we saw a herd of caribou.

We canoed across the lake and hiked up to the top of Falls Mountain. On the way up that mountain we came to a steep sheer rock face. Dick barely slowed down as he climbed around the edge of it. When he looked back and saw that I had stopped and was staring rather apprehensively at the cliff he said, "Do not take council of your fears," a famous quote from General George Patton. I told my Uncle Robert that after I returned to Iowa and he laughed and said, "Yup, that's exactly what Dick would say."

I had never been in a canoe in my life. The first day we canoed he said, "Well, if you fall out of the canoe or if the canoe overturns you'll die of exposure [because the water is so cold] before you would be able to get to ashore." Dick put me in the front of his canoe and loaded a big heavy boulder in the center. He told me that the rock gave the canoe more stability and made it less prone to tip. I don't know that he would do that when he was out alone.

I always sat in the bow of the canoe and I paddled two strokes to his one. I know that was probably the wrong thing to do but I'd take two strokes while he would take one very long stroke. He was in the stern and did all the steering. He never admonished me for doing something wrong; he just let me paddle.

One day he took me canoeing to the connecting stream between the two lakes where we fished. On my second cast I hooked a big fish on the fly rod and it was stripping line and running out into the strong current at the mouth of the stream. Dick was hollering at me and telling me what to do but I couldn't hear him over the noise of the rushing water. The fish got away. Dick walked over and said, "If you'd just taken it up around the bend there before you tried to pull it in then you wouldn't have had that problem."

I had never used a fly rod before so that was an entirely new experience for me. Fortunately, getting a fish on the line at Twin Lakes that summer was not a problem. Wherever I tossed my fly the fish were fighting over it. There were always fish and it didn't take long to catch them. We mostly caught grayling and lake trout but grayling were the most abundant and I found out later in my stay that grayling was Dick's favorite fish.

When Dick fried fish for supper he often fixed me a side dish of fireweed salad. The fireweed came from the roof of his cabin where it grew on the bed of moss that made up his "living shingles." We ate a lot of fireweed salad and fish and it was always very delicious.

For breakfast he usually fixed sourdough hotcakes topped with blueberry syrup and fried bacon. He always gave me a lot to eat and I couldn't complain about the food.

Dick had what I called a "refrigerator." It was just a wooden box that he inserted in a hole that he dug into the tundra. It had a wooden lid, which he covered with a layer of moss. He stored his bacon, eggs, cheese and other things that were perishable in there. Because they were below ground level they stayed cool.

In the evenings Dick didn't read a lot, but he was always writing in his journal or writing letters. He was just busy all the time. There wasn't ever a time that I remember while I was there that he wasn't doing something.

Dick had an outhouse but I never saw him use it and neither did I. After I returned home to Iowa someone asked me about that and I told them we went out in the woods, just like the animals.

* * *.

My grandparents lived in Iowa and Dick would always come back in the fall to stay with them. During those years my parents would take me over on weekends to visit him. I remember that Dick didn't sit in the house visiting with us for very long before he could be found outside doing chores or fixing something. Those visits were really my first opportunity to be in the outdoors. He'd take me over to Shimek [State] Forest near Farmington, Iowa and we'd get out and do a little hiking.

He always had slides of Twin Lakes to show along with his 8-millimeter films. One winter he came to my hometown in Havana, Illinois and showed his films in the basement of our Methodist church. He'd show his films of bears and moose and make a whole evening of it. We'd be there till ten or eleven o'clock at night watching films and listening to Dick's stories. He drew quite a crowd. It was free, but at the end of his presentation the congregation took up an offering to help defray his costs. Dick would give half the offering to the minister and he'd take the other half.

In the spring Dick would pack his pickup truck and head back to Alaska. He traveled back to Iowa each winter, right up to the time my grandfather passed away. My grandmother passed away first and my grandfather followed her a few years later, and after that Dick spent the winters in Alaska.

Dick was the most inquisitive person I have ever met. When I was a child and we went to Iowa to visit him for the weekend at my grandparents, he'd just pepper me with questions. He wanted to know all about my schooling and what I was studying.

One winter I spent a weekend in Iowa and I remember I had a plastic model World War II Jeep kit that one of my aunts or uncles had given me. I was too young to assemble and glue it together myself so Dick stayed up one night and put the whole thing together for me. I was astonished the next morning when I got up saw that it was completely done!

Most young boys can only wish for an uncle like Richard Proenneke. That wish came true for Dick Hackard. As a young boy his uncle became his role model and made a life-long impression. Having never traveled more than a few miles from home or flown in an airplane, he bravely left Illinois as a teenager to visit his uncle at Twin Lakes.

Let's build a raft

John Branson

I had a mark on the bank where the shallowest place on the stream was. John (Branson) removed his pants and shorts and put on his basketball shoes for the trip across. It was a long cold trip but he made it. RLP

"It looks better over here," yelled Dick as we struggled through thick dwarf birch and shoulder-high alder. It was early summer and we were hiking to Lake Clark from his cabin on Upper Twin Lake. Over halfway there on this thirty-one-mile trek we hit some very slow going as we descended toward Lachbuna Lake. I had my .338 magnum rifle with me and carried two shells in each front pocket of my shirt. The friction of alder branches hitting and gnawing at my shirt was so intense that by the time we got out of the brush there were two holes, one in each shirt pocket, and all four bullets were gone! I breathed a sigh of relief when we finally hit the shoreline where it was easy going along the beach.

We made our way toward the lower end where the lake empties into the Kijik River. A friend, Jay Mueller, lived in a cabin there. We hoped to find him home and willing to ferry us across the lake above the head of the river. It was 6 p.m. when we reached Jay's, but we found no one home. His riverboat was bottom-up and chained to a big spruce tree. The lake outlet is wide and swampy from years of beaver work and very difficult to cross. Staring at the locked boat, I recalled that I'd been in this predicament a couple of years earlier, but that time I managed to hitch a ride back to Lake Clark on a floatplane.

"Let's build a raft," said Dick. I didn't question him, it sure sounded better than heading back into the alders. We left our gear on the beach and went searching for raft logs. There were a lot of blow-down trees near the lake but the selection was not good. Most were green and heavy. "I wonder if they will float?" asked Dick as he chopped down one of the few dry-looking dead spruce we could find. We hauled the logs back to the beach, but with daylight fading we would have to wait until morning to build the raft.

We turned in early but neither of us slept well that night. After breakfast we lashed the logs together with some line that Dick had brought along. Finally, we cut two long spruce poles. At first we planned to use them as skids to move the raft into the water, and later we would use them as push poles and paddles. Not knowing how deep the raft would settle into the water, we wore our packs. We pushed offshore into deep water about 100 yards up from the head of the river. The raft settled low, it floated with only an inch of freeboard to spare! Slowly we splashed across the lake to the far shore. We secured the raft to a tree for Dick to use on his return to Twin Lakes and followed the river heading for the pass that would take us to Lake Clark. A photograph of Dick proudly standing onboard his "Tom Sawyer" raft appears in *More Readings from One Man's Wilderness*.

The first time I met Dick Proenneke was in June of 1976 when I was at Jay Hammond's homestead on the north shore of Lake Clark. Jay had asked me to build an 8-by16-foot steam bath and had lined up a good young carpenter in Port Alsworth, Ralph Nabinger, to help me. I had cut logs a year or two earlier so we were ready to build once Ralph came over. Babe Alsworth had suggested to Jay that since Ralph had never done any log work and I had done very limited log building that Dick Proenneke might be able to help us get started on it. At the time, Dick was flying his J-3 Piper Cub and he would make the trip down to Port Alsworth once a week to get his mail. If the lake was not too rough on his return trip he would land and taxi into the little bay in front of Hammond's, tie up his plane, and walk over and help Ralph and me.

Dick was an immense help on that project and I learned a thing or two, but it took a very good student to learn from him. To scribe a log he just had a little piece of wood and he used his fingers and the wood to get the distance between the logs. He had his own way of doing things, and he plunged right into them with little explanation. Sometimes I never did quite understand what he was doing. Unlike me, Ralph was innately a very good carpenter and took to the

"Proenneke system" real well. So he did the scribing and I cut out the notches. I would rough them out with a chainsaw and then chop them out with an axe and hatchet.

My most memorable time with Dick was in early July of 1979 when we hiked from Twin Lakes to Terry and Vic Gill's placer mining camp in the Bonanza Hills. It was a sixty-mile roundtrip hike that he would make several times alone during his early years at Twin Lakes. I had spent the night at his cabin, and the next morning after breakfast we loaded up the canoe and made the two-and-a-half hour paddle down to the end of the Lower Lake. We stashed the canoe under a spruce tree and took off to the west, climbing onto an escarpment of the upper terraces just north of the Chilikadrotna River. We passed by a rock that he always marveled at, a huge glacial erratic which he called "Hilton rock." It was a long trek across the high tundra until we reached what Dick called "Island Mountain" on the east edge of the Bonanza Hills. After wading across a couple of creeks we decided to lie down in the wide open to sleep for a few hours. We had traveled eleven hours nonstop and had another three to go.

Dick didn't like to camp on the long hikes I went on with him. We'd just take sleeping bags and roll them out on the tundra. I wanted to take our rest stop in the timber but Dick wanted to climb up the side of the mountain where the bugs wouldn't be as bad. It was not a peaceful rest stop. The breeze that we gained by being higher up on the slope did little to discourage the bugs. It began sprinkling and that soon gave way to a light rain. Around three in the morning, I started to get very cold. Dick suggested that "We might just as well be walking as suffering." It was still light, so we got up and took off. Fog and light rain made for some very wet brush.

It was hard to see, but Dick knew the way and after about three hours we arrived at the Gills'. I don't know what time it was but it must have been early morning. The smoke was coming out of their stovepipe; they knew we were coming but not the exact day. I think they were getting up pretty early every morning just in case we'd arrive. They were very happy to see us and we were very happy to have a roof over our heads. I took a nap and then split some wood while Dick went with Terry to solve a problem with the brakes on their John Deere dozer.

The Gills always had a backlog of mechanical problems for Dick to solve and he stayed until everything was shipshape and running. Dick had gone to a diesel mechanic's school in Portland in the late 1940s. He went in as a student and he came out as an instructor. He was very smart and methodical. It seemed like he and his brothers inherited some of their mechanical skills from their father. As a father and sons team they used to restore barns and houses, drill wells, and repair farm machinery. Ironically, he dropped out of high school after his sophomore year. Had he come from a different background he might have gone on to become an engineer or a doctor.

I heard the dozer shut down, and soon Dick and Terry came walking back to the cabin. As usual Dick worked his magic, applying some penetrating oil and a few gentle blows with a hammer, and he had the dozer turning on a dime. After a good supper we turned in to rest up for the long hike back to Twin Lakes.

At 8 a.m. the next day we said our good-byes and climbed the high ridge behind the Gills' camp. Going was good, cool with a nice breeze at our backs. Noon saw us back on Island Mountain. Dick was not an extremely fast hiker, but he was incredibly steady and relentless. When I needed to relieve myself he never stopped, and when he had to do likewise he would just do so and resume his steady pace. He never took a conventional backpack, instead he used a pack frame, which had a little can hanging from it that he could use to dip drinking water. He would also tie on a blanket or sleeping bag and an ammo pouch that he'd fill with food—candy bars and rolled up pancakes with peanut butter, his so called "sticks of dynamite."

We retraced our route across the open tundra and dropped into the timber with another hour to go before we reached the lower lake. Across from us on an open ridge was a good-sized brown bear and he was coming our way. We watched as he entered some heavy brush on a slope facing us, and then just as quickly he took off on a dead run into the trees where we were headed. A short while later we entered the timber and sure enough, we crossed his trail because there was a pile of fresh bear scat still steaming. Dick stopped, looked back at me and said, "You better jack a shell into that 30.06, boy, that bear might be right around here." I quickly responded and chambered a round. We never did see that bear, but we quickened our pace and kept an eye on our flank for the next half mile. We arrived back at the canoe making the hike in just over eleven hours— according to Dick, his fastest time ever.

We had a nice tail wind on the paddle back up the lake, and we made it to Dick's cabin in two hours and twenty minutes. Dick was an exacting canoeist. He would not let anyone paddle stern but himself. If you messed up and hit the side of the canoe or hit the water with the tip of your paddle on the backstroke too often, he'd say, "Come on, you can do better than that." He was a perfectionist, and I always sensed that he was watching to see if I measured up to his standards.

The fall before that hike Jay Hammond had me get a gang of guys together to cut logs for an addition to Jay's main cabin and a combination woodshed-generator building. We went across Lake Clark and found a good stand of spruce east of the mouth of Current Creek. We set up a temporary camp and stayed there for three days. Dick came down to join us, but he wouldn't stay in our big wall tent. Instead he crawled underneath a great big spruce tree and rolled up in a sleeping bag and some canvas. Dick stayed like that in spite of the fact that we had light snow a few mornings. A very light sleeper, he preferred to face the elements rather than the prospect of being kept awake by the activity inside the tent.

Every morning we'd get a big fire going and after breakfast we'd cut trees, limb them, and cut out the logs we needed. Dick was in his element, he was such a good woodsman trimming them up. He showed us how to cut knobs off the trees just the right way so you didn't pull out a big chunk of wood. We cut all the logs that we needed and had a lot of fun in the process.

I knew Dick for over two decades, and I treasure the times we spent together. Dick was competitive by nature and at times a bit of a rivalry developed between us. We may not have always agreed on the best route through the alder brush or the best candidates in the presidential elections, but any disagreements that we had were always friendly and over the years forgotten or forgiven.

John Branson has been a historian for Lake Clark National Park and Preserve for over 25 years. He is known for his relentless pursuit of old photographs and has written numerous books on the history of the area. He has also edited three volumes covering eighteen years of Dick Proenneke's journals. Branson serves as an authority and guide for archeologists and native Alaskans who wish to visit the Kijik National Historic Landmark and the Telaquana Trail, a historic Dena'ina Athabascan route from Telaquana Lake to Kijik Village on Lake Clark.

My stepfather remarked that Dick looked like he was made of wire

Craig Coray

June 28. I was eating supper when there came a light rap on the door. The first time anyone had knocked on my door for a year or more. It was Craig Coray from Lake Clark. RLP

I first heard of Dick Proenneke in 1968 from my friends, the Alsworth boys, who lived down lake from me on Lake Clark. But it wasn't until almost a decade later, in 1977, that I actually met Dick. I had just completed a hike from Lachbuna Lake to Twin Lakes, accompanied by John Branson and Heidi Hammond. Dick graciously set us up with a cabin to stay in. My first impression was of a very competent wilderness dweller, who belonged there every bit as much as the wild creatures around him. They provided him with companionship that was at least as important as what he got from his less frequent human encounters. Dick was a great host and loved to share his experiences and his lifestyle, yet I had the distinct impression that rather than craving human company, he could take it or leave it.

He didn't have a radio and didn't ask for news of the outside world—in fact he made it plain that he got along quite well without it. So although nowhere close to a misanthrope, Dick definitely lived in his own world. I have known a number of old-timers from the Lake Clark area—men who for one reason or another seemed to prefer living outside the constraints of society. Inevitably these men were maladjusted in one way or another, often given to behavior that could have gotten them arrested had there been law enforcement around. In this context I had to wonder about Dick—what was he escaping from? If there was anything in his character that might have suggested such, it was not readily apparent. It seemed that he just liked being alone, in a world of pristine beauty, in the company of wild things. Possibly he felt disillusionment with humanity. If so he didn't talk about it.

In my experience he wasn't much given to philosophizing, and in that sense was no Alaskan Thoreau. He certainly possessed and practiced a strong wilderness ethic, yet he didn't really preach it and did not have the scientific background to incorporate it into a broader ecological perspective. His gift was that of a keen observer of natural phenomena. He was also a gifted wildlife photographer, possessing a great deal of patience, which is the most crucial component to success in that field. His expertise at carpentry, using the most limited tools and materials, is legendary, and of that he was justifiably proud.

On our return journey to Lake Clark, John and I were accompanied by Leon Alsworth—just a boy then—and Dick himself, who led us up and through a pass that dropped down into the Kijik River Drainage. I believe he called this False Pass. Like the other old-timers with whom I hiked as a boy—Brown Carlson and Joe Thompson—Dick's pace was more steady than fast, although he was by no means slow. He didn't say much while he walked, probably too keen on observing what might be missed if given to such distractions. At the top of the pass we went our separate ways.

My next encounter with Dick was a year later, when I flew into Twin Lakes with my brother David and his friend Marilyn. I had tried to get word to Dick that we were coming, but the dates were uncertain and I think we surprised him. Once again he was a gracious host. We spent the night in one of Spike's cabins and Dick helped us plan a hike to the sheep lick across the lake. The next day he ferried us across in his canoe. I don't recall a lot about this visit except that Dick was having a full scale war with porcupines.

I saw Dick again briefly that summer when he and John Branson walked into my yard at Lake Clark, having just hiked down from Twin Lakes. It was pouring rain and he and John were unbelievably wet. The water was coming off their cuffs in streams. I offered them a boat ride to Miller Creek, but they were determined to walk the rest of the way. My stepfather remarked that Dick looked like he was made of wire.

The last time I saw him was at Jay Hammond's place on Miller Creek many years later. At that time I believe he was no longer staying at

Twin. He informed me that he'd had a mini stroke and that although he was doing okay it had affected his memory. I asked him when the stroke had taken place and he replied, with a touch of humor tinged with irony, that the funny thing about it was that he couldn't remember.

I greatly admired Dick's lifestyle and his handiwork. He made the best sourdough pancakes ever and his beans were pretty good too. He had taken the concept of simple living to an art. I remember him demonstrating the advantages of a gravel floor, which instead of sweeping he cleaned with a rake. Later I was told that someone had talked him into putting carpet down over the gravel because it would be nicer on his feet. If I remember correctly the carpet absorbed moisture and didn't last long after he moved out of the cabin.

Craig Coray is a longtime resident of Lake Clark where he has lived off and on since 1958 when his parents first homesteaded at Portage Creek. Craig taught music theory and northern indigenous music at the University of Alaska Anchorage. He is considered by many to be Alaska's most authentic classical composer.

Have you ever seen a dipper nest

Stu Ramstad

April 5, 1978. A plane circled and landed. Only the pilot got out to meet me. He introduced himself as Stu Ramstad from Fishtrap Lake. We stood on the ice in the warm sun and visited. Stu in his short sleeves and wearing well-worn out cowboy boots. RLP

I visited Dick Proenneke many times over the years, but one day stands out above all the rest. Early that day I flew folk singer and recording artist John Denver to the Newhalen River below Lake Clark, where we planned to join up with river guide Cliff Pulis. At the time, John was producing a film entitled "Let There Be A Voice" for the Nature Series on U.S. Public Television.

Cliff picked us up at Lake Iliamna and took us upriver in his jet boat. He liked to give his passengers a thrill by abruptly pulling his boat up under a small waterfall and letting the water cascade onto the covered deck and windshield. Then he would turn to his passengers and say, "Now this is a waterfall!"

I'd gotten a bath once before when he did this trick so I knew enough to stand in the stern of the boat. While John and I were looking at the waterfall we saw a dipper fly right through the falling water and disappear behind it. We thought it must have had a nest in the rocks behind the falls.

Later that day we flew up Dick's to visit and had a cup of tea. John brought along herbal tea and a flask of maple syrup which Dick seemed to enjoy. We mentioned the experience that we had earlier in the day on the boat when the dipper flew through the waterfall.

Dick perked up with a twinkle in his eyes and asked, "Have you ever seen a dipper nest?" We shook our heads and said no. Immediately he jumped up, went outside, and erected the ladder to his cache. John and I followed and stood behind his cabin. He climbed up that ladder quicker than a red squirrel and came down holding what looked like a well-used softball with a hole in it. He walked over to us and said, "This is a dipper nest."

He never elaborated as to how he came by the nest. After admiring the nest for a few minutes we handed it back to him. He climbed back up the ladder and returned it to the cache.

After that we said our goodbyes, posed for a photograph, and climbed back in the floatplane. As I was warming up the engine and taxing out for departure John turned to me and said, in his typical dialect, "What a far out little guy."

Aviator, guide, and third generation Alaskan Stu Ramstad became a pilot at the age of fourteen in 1954. He has overcome many exciting challenges in over forty years of flying through the mountains between Anchorage and his Little Mulchatna Lodge on Fishtrap Lake, including two in-flight fires.

You kids Ok in there

Jerry and Norma Holt

August 18, 1971. Going up the creek trail and I bumped into a rooster grouse. A few feet of precious film wasted there. On up and I heard a plane – a twin engine and there came a red and white [Widgeon] up the left side over the mountains. A Kodiak Airway, that would be Jerry [Holt] and family. Much racket on the waterfront and I found them at my beach unable to get out of the water and sitting at a cockeyed angle. RLP

We had our float plane, an Aeronca Sedan, pulled up on the beach near Dick Proenneke's cabin. The wind had been rather light that morning but suddenly it picked up from the east and was blowing down lake. Within what seemed like a few minutes it was gusting over forty miles per hour, and large whitecaps began pounding the beach. The Aeronca, parked crosswise to the wind, began rocking violently. I was frantically struggling to do anything I could to tie it down because I feared that it could flip over.

I looked up and saw Dick walking toward me, "Let me show you how to do that," he said. With me still hanging onto the tail rope, Dick quickly secured a rope to the wing facing into the wind and placed a second rope on the front cleat of the starboard float. He said, "Ok, now push it off." I pushed off and Dick tossed me one of the ropes he was holding. Together we pulled the nose into the wind and secured the ropes. We held it there until the wind died a while later. At the time I didn't know that Dick had any experience with airplanes. I was amazed at how quickly he sized up the situation and came up with a solution. He saved our airplane.

We planned to spend a month at Twin Lakes that year with our two sons, doing some fishing and hiking. For part of that time Dick guided us around and invited us to his cabin. We got a kick out of the way he moved in that country—like a mountain goat. He'd bend over while walking, and without breaking a stride he'd reach down and grab a handful of blueberries. He moved fast when he was alone, but when he was with us and the boys he would say, "We'll just take it easy, we'll just go one step at a time and enjoy the scenery."

Hiking with Dick was more than a walk up the valley or the side of a mountain. He told us about the different berries and other plants that we were seeing so that by the end of the hike he had given us a lesson on what grew up there.

When it was time to return to Kodiak, Jerry made one trip with our oldest son but then couldn't pick our younger son and me up for a week or more due to weather. Dick used to check on us every day. He'd come by and he'd ask, "You kids okay in there?" He'd make sure that we always had enough to eat: sourdough pancakes, fireweed salad, and beans. He always had beans.

I remember that he became very protective of the animals. Having shared the winter with them, he had a lot of compassion for them. The second time that we visited I shot a caribou and he helped me skin it out. And we spent some time. We took very good care of the meat and did the fleshing of the hide and all that business, making sure every scrap was used. I also learned that Dick could pack. He put a load on his back, and at his age I was surprised that he could do it.

Dick was not real happy with a local guide. He'd go up the mountain and Dick would hear a shot up there and he'd figure, *well, all right, they've got one down*. He'd wait for them to come down the mountain then he'd go up the trail and find what they had left, which was way more than they should have. And he'd pack the rest of the meat down and he'd dry it. He used to set up a kind of a tepee. He used some plastic sheeting and to wrap around it and make himself a smoker. He really considered that place and the animals his responsibility. He made sure they were treated right.

Dick was a unique character, and I've never known anyone quite like him. He loved his solitude but he wasn't standoffish or a recluse. He was sociable. He took pride in being able to do what he did: build his cabin, be self-sufficient, observe and photograph wildlife, and thrive, even during the long, harsh winter months. He was certainly at home there at Twin Lakes and he truly loved the land.

Jerry Holt met Dick Proenneke in the late 1950s when he was working as a security officer at the Kodiak Naval Base. An aircraft mechanic and a gemologist with a passion for gold nuggets, it's easy to understand why he and Dick quickly became friends. After Jerry learned to fly, he bought an old Aeronca Sedan on floats that he and Norma flew to Twin Lakes to visit their good friend Dick.

No, I'll walk around and down

Leon Alsworth III

"I was just finishing dishes when I heard a plane and it sounded like the easy running T-Craft. Sure enough - a pass overhead - a turn down country and he came in to the beach. I could see heads of two little boys over the bottom of the window. At last Leon & Sig had arrived at Twin Lakes. Babe turned her around and tied the tail to a tree. Out came the little guys with their sleeping bags. Babe unloaded their luggage and a big plastic garbage bag, four dozen eggs, and a slab of bacon. "Feed them lots of smoked fish," he said."
RLP

I grew up with my grandparents in Port Alsworth during the 1960s and 1970s. My first memory of Dick is seeing him in coveralls driving the grader. Nobody else wore coveralls at that time and nobody else ran that grader, so whenever I heard the grader running I knew Dick was here. I didn't realize it at the time but the reason he wore coveralls was that greasing that old grader and tinkering around with it was a very messy job.

I was always impressed with the grader. It was big, old, and rusty. One day I asked Dick, "How much longer is this grader going to run?" He said, "It could quit at any time and never run again." But it actually ran long after Dick stopped maintaining it. When he finished grading the airstrip he usually turned his attention to the garden. He used the old Ford tractor to work up the garden for planting in the spring and in the fall he would help dig potatoes.

A few years after he built his cabin at Twin Lakes my grandfather (Babe) would take my brother Sig and me up during the summer to stay with him for a week at a time. I can still remember what a special event it was for us. He treated us like grandchildren and always had something planned. We'd eat breakfast and then we'd head out, either on a hike up a mountain or a paddle up or down the lake in the canoe. One trip we really enjoyed was when he took us up to the head of the lake where there's a black sand beach and we got to pan out a bunch of black sand. It was great fun for two young boys.

We did a lot of hiking and I always wanted to be out in front or try to keep ahead. We may have had short legs, but we had a lot of energy. I don't ever remember getting tired out hiking with Dick; part of the reason is that he would slow down for us and we'd occasionally stop to look at sheep or bears. But I did get plenty worn out on a hike we took from Twin Lakes to Lachbuna Lake with John Branson.

Dick liked to play tricks on us. One day when we were on a hike he told us he was expecting John Branson to be hiking up from Lake Clark to see him. Sig and I were walking along behind Dick when suddenly he stopped, pointed to a distant ridge and said, "There's John over there." We looked and looked and were pretty well convinced that it was John standing up there on the skyline. We continued walking up the slope in that direction but as we got closer it became clear that it was a rock spire sticking up.

For someone accustomed to living alone, it must have been a shock for Dick to suddenly have two young rambunctious boys under foot. We started out sleeping on the lower bunk in his cabin but after a couple nights of whispering and giggling we got moved outside into a tent. The second year we came up he just led us straight to the tent. On one hike Sig and I started to roll rocks down the side of a mountain, a game that Dick did not appreciate. And I remember us constantly asking, "Hey, can we go to the top of that mountain?" Sometimes Dick would just let us head off, knowing that after a short distance we'd realize that mountaintop was farther away than we could hike in several days.

One summer Dick taught us a song. Its lyrics contained all the different branches of the military. Dick tape-recorded my brother and me singing the song and he sent copies of it to friends and relatives. Two of the verses were:

The biscuits in the Army
They say are mighty fine.

One rolled off the table
And hurt a friend of mine.

They say that in the Navy,
The coffee's mighty fine
it looks like muddy water
And tastes like turpentine

There were many more lines but I don't remember them all. The Navy verse was followed by one from the Air Force.

* * *

When I started work as a pilot-ranger for Lake Clark National Park and Preserve in the late 1980s I inherited a role that my grandfather (Babe) and Uncle Glen (Alsworth) had filled since the time Dick first arrived at Twin Lakes in 1967—flying up to check on Dick and deliver his mail and supplies. As a backcountry park volunteer, Dick was very much a part of the staff.

Most of my flights to Twin Lakes were in the Park's Cessna 185 which had a tail number ending in eight, seven, N [Pronounced November for clarity over the radio]. Dick must have seen that plane hundreds of times over the years, but when he hailed it on the radio he called the numbers in sequence "Seven, Eight, November." I don't know when he started doing it but he had the numbers backwards. I always got a kick out of that.

Flights up to Twin Lakes were sometimes routine, occasionally dangerous, and often filled with the unexpected. I recall one time in early spring when I flew up with the Piper Super Cub. Dick had some mail that he was very anxious to send out. As I circled above his cabin I could see that the ice was breaking up and going out near the head of the lake. I don't know if he could see it, but he kept insisting that the ice was fine in front of his cabin. Finally I said, "Ok, I'll land and grab your mail but I will not shut down the engine." When I landed and stopped in front of his beach Dick positioned himself in front of the left wing and grabbed ahold of the strut. I stayed in the pilot's seat with the engine running as Dick visited like we had all the time in the world. When I returned the next day the entire lake was free of ice, including where I was sitting hours earlier.

I learned to be skeptical of Dick's assessment of lake ice. He usually seemed to think the ice was better than it was. "Oh, yeah, the ice is fine," he'd say. And then I'd land and I'd be able to put my foot through somewhere. More than once I remember him talking about walking on the ice and having to quicken his pace because he was falling through.

Dick usually had something he was anxious to show me or tell me about, especially wildlife sightings. If the spotting scope was out and set up when I arrived I knew that something exciting was happening on one of the nearby mountain slopes. One morning when he greeted me he said, "Oh, boy, take a look at this." The spotting scope was pointed at a slope across the lake. I looked in the scope and saw a lynx feeding on a Dall sheep. Dick said it had killed the sheep high on the mountainside. Not only had I never seen that before, I would never have expected that a lynx was capable of taking down an adult sheep, especially in the high alpine where sheep have the advantage of maneuvering on steep terrain.

When I took off in the plane I flew over and circled the kill site. From the tracks in the snow, I could see that the lynx had come across a ridge top and spooked two sheep that were on a steep slope below it. One animal bolted, circled around the lynx, and headed upslope. The other animal ran downslope. The lynx pursued the animal that ran downslope and evidently overtook it when the sheep hit some deep snow. It was a big lynx and it remained there feeding on the sheep while I circled.

One thing was consistent about visiting Dick; I could always count on leaving with a big stack of outgoing letters. Dick would often be sealing letters in envelopes as I was walking toward the door to leave. His outgoing and incoming mail followed a cyclic pattern. After I hauled out a big sack of his letters one week, I could count on returning with an equal or even larger sack of letters a couple weeks later. I don't remember him ordering much through the mail but people would send him boxes at all times of the year.

One year Patty Brown wrote Dick and told him about a fancy dress that she had recently worn to a dinner party. Patty knew Dick well, having spent quite a bit of time with him while working as a seasonal employee of the Park. In his next letter Dick responded, "Oh, I wish I could have seen it." To Dick's surprise, she wrote back and said, "I'll wear that dress to Twin Lakes for you."

Patty flew out to Port Alsworth and asked me to fly her up to Twin Lakes. At the time I had a Super Cub on wheels. She put on this nice dress and climbed into the back of my Cub. Once we were in the air, we called on the radio and asked Dick to meet us at a rough strip at the head of the lake. When we arrived we saw Dick's canoe pulled up on the beach and him standing nearby. I landed and she promptly hopped out of the Cub in her fancy black dress.

A few days later I picked her up at Dick's beach but I never did hear if she wore that dress when they paddled back down lake. I think I can safely say that this was the first and only time that a woman in an evening dress met Dick at the head of upper Twin Lake.

Dick was always very interested in aircraft, and I was one of his principle sources of information. Whenever a plane went down near Twin Lakes Dick was among the first on the scene. One year a Luscombe [aircraft] went down near the south end of Low Pass after it encountered low visibility. Dick had already visited the crash site but he wanted to take me there. It was early spring and the pass was still mostly covered with snow. The snow was crusty though, and we were able to walk in without snowshoes. It was a nostalgic hike because I'd made it many times with Dick, including the day that he tried to convince my younger brother Sig and me that a rock spire was John Branson.

After spending some time looking at the plane wreckage we headed back through the pass toward Upper Twin Lake. We ascended to the pass on Dick's normal route, an old caribou trail that arches around a rockslide and gently gains elevation. As we headed down I noticed that there was a big, drifted snow pack covering the creek drainage. It extended from the top of the pass almost a third of the way to the lakeshore. I was sure I could make quick time by sliding down the snow and invited Dick to join me. Without hesitation he said, "Nooo. I'll walk around and down."

In all the years that I hiked with Dick this was one of the few times that I walked straight and he didn't. Dick was known for his long straight marches across the lakes and up the valleys in winter. Dick said to me once, "You've got to look ahead at something way up and march straight at it." It seemed like he felt a straight line on the snow was a necessity to keep things neat. It was the same when we paddled a canoe. It had to be straight. He would take a line-of-sight and paddle straight ahead. No zigzagging. [Editor's Note: Dick was cautious on snow-covered slopes and felt that it was too risky to glissade down the slope as Leon did.]

Leon Alsworth was introduced to Dick Proenneke when his grandfather brought him out of the wilderness to plant potatoes and grade a runway. As a young boy, a highlight of his summer was spending a week with Dick at his cabin. After Leon became a pilot-ranger for the National Park Service, he would return the favor. Dick was always anxiously awaiting his arrival at Twin Lakes. Together they went on hikes, kept track of the local wolf pack, checked on visitors, ran a snow survey course, and compared notes on the season's blueberry crop. Leon accompanied Dick on his final canoe paddle in 2000, but not unlike when he was a boy, Dick sat in the stern, and steered a straight course.

It helps settle the estate if you have a body

Jill Acheson

June 26. As I got closer I could make out strange uniforms moving through the trees. Maybe it was BLM in for a check up on the legality of my cabin. ... When I got closer I saw a slim guy with a crumpled cowboy hat. Bob Acheson formerly of Kodiak and now Ellensburg, Washington. I was surprised and glad to see the guy. RLP

Seasonally, in early September in the 1980s, at the end of set gill-netting on Kodiak Island, I would fly out to Twin Lakes to stay in the cabins my father, Bob Acheson, had purchased from Spike and Hope Carrithers. I went to hike, to pick blueberries and cranberries, and to visit Dick, with whom our family had been friends since his Kodiak days.

Prizing out stories from these memories of Dick and of Twin Lakes has given me such pleasure. Just remembering how glad I was to see the familiar lake come into view after a flight through Lake Clark Pass, or sometimes over the top makes me feel young again!

Sometimes I came to Twin Lakes alone, and other times I met family or a friend, but every time it was wonderful to hike or canoe with Dick and to be, for a short time, a part of one man's wilderness. Hiking up Hope Creek to the Graveyard of Stones, or "around the mountain," or picking berries at Fox Ponds on the Lower Lake, or canoeing across the lake to hike Falls Mountain, or up the lake to go to the glacier, all were adventures. Even short hikes to Teetering Rock or Split Rock came with the thrill of seeing caribou, sheep, moose or bear and with the stories and observations of Dick's years of living there.

Sitting with him, soaking our bare feet in Glacier Creek after a hike on the glacier, I listened to Dick as he remembered the big ram that had died in a rock slide on the moraine. Dick had admired the full curl horns and salvaged them. His respect for that ram and the way he felt about the horns was much more moving than the trophy hunter's attitude towards their kill of a "big one." Dick's knowledge of and respect for the real residents of Twin Lakes inspires and informs me still.

In 1987, during a week my brother, Rob Acheson, and my late husband, Jim Mahik, and I spent at Twin Lakes, we had a memorable adventure on the lake. We left with Dick, all four of us in the canoe, to paddle across the sunny calm lake to hike up Falls Mountain. It was a beautiful hike up the canyon by the falls, seeing sheep and lambs and then the great views of the country from Roy Allen's Peak. As we made our steep way down the mountain, a worrying wind blew up, white-capping the lake, making it lumpy (as we say in Moser Bay when fishing!). To canoe back over the lake with all four of us was clearly unwise.

Rob and I, like Dick, were smallish, but Jim, though lean, was 6 ft. 4 in., the obvious one to leave behind! With warm clothes, snacks, and his camera, Jim was content to wait as long as it took for the lake to calm down. I lay down in the canoe as directed, and Rob and Dick, keeping low, paddled us safely back. Rob and I were, of course, wearing life jackets, as Dick always said it helps settle the estate if you have a body.

Despite the increasing roughness of the lake, Dick was not content to leave Jim on the other side. Uncharacteristically for him (Dick was not a motor man) Dick put the small, old outboard on the canoe and went back for Jim. In later years, both Jim and Rob would exclaim over the severity of the lake's conditions, and that day Rob and I watched the long slow progress of the canoe, wondering what we would do if we saw it start to capsize. Not to worry, they came back safely; Dick crouched by the motor, and Jim's six-foot-four self lying down on the canoe bottom, in a life jacket, with his hand crossed over his chest.

We truly enjoyed our dinner that night: fresh corn on the cob and New York steaks all around (brought by Rob from the ranch in Ellensburg, WA). And we celebrated Dick's toughness and skill with a Coke toast!

In 1996 Rob and his wife, Louise and our sister Carolyn, and I made a sentimental journey to our Alaska beginnings in Flat, AK. We flew from Flat over the mountains and wide river valleys and into Twin Lakes for another good visit with Dick.

In 1998, on our last visit with Dick in Twin Lakes, Rob, his son Charlie, and I flew in on our way to Kodiak. Although Dick leaned more heavily on his walking stick, his pace was steady, and the sound of his whistle and pleasant humming is with me still.

I've been back to Twin Lakes three times since Dick's been gone. The care and skill of Kay and Monroe's efforts with upkeep at Twin Lakes is wonderful—Spike and Hope's cabins are perfection. And Dick's cabin, raked beach, canoe, and chair at the water is just as Dick would like it. It was easy to imagine (except for the absence of the log bridge) that I'd meet Dick on the path as I walked to Hope Creek with my water buckets.

In the 1930's Jill Acheson's father worked for the U.S. Geodetic Survey (USGS) on a project to map the coast of Alaska. He became fond of Kodiak Island and opened a general store after leaving USGS. It was here that he met the Carrithers. Later, he would purchase Spike's and Hopes Cabin, paving the way for Jill to meet Dick and have those memorable hikes at Twin Lakes.

Not exactly, but I just about was run over by one once

Stu Coleman

August 1, 1979. Overcast, light breeze up and 49 degrees. Strange tracks on my beach and the door latch handle not at the angle I had left it. On the table a big package and a few letters with a note on top. It read- Dick, Brought your mail from Port Alsworth. Sorry I missed you. I am a temporary National Park Service ranger assigned to Lake Clark this summer. Will try to stop back at a later date. Stu Coleman. So, the ranger was here. I would like to hear what he has to say but to catch me home he had better come pretty early or late if it is a day to travel. RLP

I was naturally curious about a man that settled into a remote area of Alaska and built a log cabin that was the epitome of workmanship and efficiency. I couldn't even imagine what stories he could tell me about the adventures he had experienced. After I got to know Dick Proenneke I found him to be modest and not the least bit boastful or pretentious. But I was able, on occasion, to illicit some striking stories. Like the time I asked him if he had ever been attacked by a grizzly bear? He said, "No, not exactly, but I just about was run over by one once!"

Dick leaned back in his chair and told me about the day he was hiking near a mining camp in the Bonanza Hills. He was hoping to see a big moose he knew was in the area. He followed a caribou trail down a brushy hillside and when he heard a rustle in the brush assumed that it was his moose. But when he looked up, it wasn't a moose. It was a big brown bear.

The bear was traveling faster than a trot and closing the distance fast. Dick didn't have a gun so he started to yell and wave his arms. While he was hastily backing up he tripped and fell to the ground. Dick said he was lying flat on his back kicking at the bear's nose with both feet. To Dick's surprise the bear turned and ran back over the same trail Dick had just climbed. According to Dick, the bear didn't look back.

Dick figured that because he was hiking into a light headwind the bear did not detect his scent until he was virtually on top of him. Once he did, he recognized that this small kicking animal was not game and potentially a threat. Dick was very comfortable in bear country, not cavalier, but respectful and always cautious.

I first met Dick in the summer of 1979. I was one of nineteen National Park Service Rangers from the "Lower 48" that were selected and sent to Alaska to watch over the new National Park Service Monuments that had been withdrawn by former President Jimmy Carter. I was at the Great Smoky Mountains National Park as the Chief of Natural and Cultural Resources when I received the call.

Forty-eight million acres had been designated by the President in one fell swoop, basically doubling the area managed by the National Park Service and breaking a deadlock on the division of federal lands that had existed since Alaska became our 49th state. There was quite a cloud of suspicion and yes, intense dislike, of the National Park Service (NPS) and of Park Rangers, who represented NPS in the field. We were met with an air of disrespect and uncooperativeness by State representatives and Alaskans on the ground. Certainly it was the first time in my Park Service career that I was cast in a black rather than a white hat!

I was no stranger to Alaska, having served two years in the U.S. Army as a Chemical, Biological, and Radiological Officer for the 171st Infantry Brigade at Fort Wainwright near Fairbanks. The Fairbanks area is a far cry from the Lake Clark country in both geographic relief and wildlife. My assignment at Lake Clark was a totally new Alaska experience for me.

During the summer of 1979 I was the first and only field ranger assigned to the 1.6 million-acre Lake Clark National Monument and 1.4 million-acre Preserve. In briefings on my new assignment, I was told about a man that lived on the upper end of two lakes referred to as Twin Lakes. But aside from what I heard, I knew very little about this individual by the name of Proenneke.

My quarters were in a rented cabin on a small island near Port Alsworth. I shared my cabin with a pilot from the federal Office of Aircraft Services. For transportation we had a Cessna 185 on floats, a 21-foot

Boston Whaler with twin 85 horsepower outboards, and a rubber Zodiac raft with a small outboard motor. My principle assignment was to patrol the new Monument and to make personal contacts. It was important to inform and educate the public about the new Monument and what the changes in land status meant to them. That was easier said than done, as I found out.

During my patrols we flew over and landed at Twin Lakes a number of times during the summer. I was told that if Dick "liked you and accepted you" he would invite you in for a cup of tea! I was not sure that was true, but in those early visits I hoped it was. My first meetings with Dick were a bit formal because a certain amount of posturing by both of us was going on. I am sure Dick was probably wondering just what was in store for him and his cabin in this new National Monument. He knew this was coming for some time, and I'm sure there were many rumors floating around. By the third visit he invited me to have a cup of tea with him and the courtesy was extended in every visit thereafter. I think we both recognized that we were on the same side concerning the protection and preservation of the wildlife and natural resources in the new Monument and Preserve.

We settled into a relationship of mutual trust and respect and I enjoyed the man immensely. As the summer progressed, we talked about people, places, and Park Service policy. Illegal hunting was one of the major concerns at the time. From Dick I learned which hunters needed to be watched more closely, and I in turn would ask him about people I met while on patrol. I found him to be very honest and sincere in his evaluations and appreciated his perspective.

When I reported back to Anchorage, I told my superiors that Dick was exactly the kind of person the NPS wanted on the ground in this newly created Monument. In fact, before I departed Lake Clark, Dick asked me what I thought the NPS was going to do about him since he was basically a squatter. I told him I thought the agency would either appoint him as a volunteer and require him to live in his cabin or would allow him to live where he was and charge him a rental fee of $1.00 a year for the quarters. And I reported to Anchorage exactly what I had told Dick.

* * *

Dick always left a map of the area on the cabin table and a flagged pin to show exactly where he intended to go that day. To my knowledge the cabin door was never locked. I asked him why he placed the pin on the map and he jokingly responded, "So if anyone is interested enough they would know where to look for my body!" On a more serious note, visitors who had business with him might also know where he was and perhaps how long he might be gone. The map was so full of holes from past pin placements that it literally looked like one of those old-time punchboards.

I remarked one time about how clean his cabin's gravel floor was. He said, "Well, you arrived just after spring cleaning." "How so," I asked. Dick explained that he scooped up the gravel from the floor one bucket-full at a time, took it to the lake shore, washed it, and spread it back on the floor of the cabin. As you can imagine, it took a number of trips. In between washings he swept the floor with a broom.

He followed the practice of WASTE-NOT-WANT-NOT. Once when we visited I noticed a fish line extended into the lake with what appeared to fish intestines carefully threaded on the hook. I asked him why he was using intestines for bait. He said that he had caught a lake trout that morning and rather than throw the insides away he put them on a hook and figured he would catch a burbot for yet another meal.

Dick was a master of fashioning containers and tools from wood and metal. Discarded tin gas cans made all kinds of useful containers, patches, traps, and tools. He selected tree knots and made all sorts of useful articles such as stirring spoons and ladles. He really was quite talented in that regard.

When I left Lake Clark at the end of the summer and I returned home to Tennessee and the Great Smokys, I made up a large package of assorted teas and sent him a surprise bundle with a thank you for helping to educate this Park Ranger. I considered it an honor to have met and spent some time with this remarkable man.

During the summer of 1979, when nineteen Park Service Rangers from the Lower 48 headed out into the newly created Alaska National Monuments, they were rarely invited in for tea. Stu Coleman was one of the lucky ones, because Dick Proenneke lived in his assigned Monument. When Stu travelled to Anchorage for treatment of an impacted tooth, the first dentist he visited said that he would prefer not to treat a National Park Service employee. Stu recently retired after spending his final years working with bison and bears at Yellowstone.

How could that man restore an aluminum canoe at Twin Lakes

Paul Haertel

October 12. Paul said "How about us leaving you a walkie talkie for the winter. If we come you can advise us of the condition of the ice or if the batteries at the repeater on the mt. peak in the volcanics are warm enough you can call Park Service headquarters at Port Alsworth". They would give me two batteries to be sure I had enough power here. To me it would be like using the kicker on the canoe. More of a challenge without it. He insisted that I take it and use it if the need was there. So - they showed me how it worked and so tonight I could turn it on and talk to anyone who happens to be in the big log house at headquarters at the narrows leading to Babes Bay.

In all of the time that I spent in the National Park Service, which spanned about forty-one years and spanned the continent from Alaska to Maine, I never quite met a person like Dick Proenneke. He was talented in so many ways. He could make or repair just about anything, and it seemed to me that he could operate any piece of machinery put in front of him. And if that weren't enough, he had a passionate interest in all that surrounded him: the wildlife, vegetation, weather, geology, glaciers and all else that comprised the wilderness in which he lived.

I don't think I ever visited with him when he didn't ask a question that was really challenging. And it always had something to do with what he was observing. His ability to live alone and still be so welcoming and friendly was just incredible.

In 1978, prior to the official designation of Lake Clark National Park and Preserve, I made a trip to Twin Lakes along with other staff from the Washington and Alaska Offices of the National Park Service. We landed at Twin Lakes in a Grumman Goose and had a fine visit with

Dick. Afterward, as the pilot powered up the Goose to turn lake-ward and pull away from the beach, one of the fellows looked back and saw Dick's canoe flying through the air. That made everybody sick because we'd just had this wonderful visit with him and then our prop wash blew his canoe into the rocks.

We immediately turned around, taxied back, and shut down. The canoe was badly dented in several places. Dick Stenmark, who was then in the Washington office and who would later became Alaska Region Deputy Regional Director, told Dick that we would make that right to him no matter what it took. Less than a week later Stu Coleman flew up to Dick's with Bill Belinsky, who was the Office of Aircraft Services pilot assigned there at that time. To their absolute amazement, his canoe was perfectly restored. Now, how could that man restore an aluminum canoe at Twin Lakes?

We issued Dick a park service radio and that proved to be of immense help to Mike Tolleffson, the Chief Ranger at that time. Dick called in on the radio one day and said that he'd heard an airplane land and he'd heard shots. He thought that a moose had been killed illegally on Upper Twin Lake. We wouldn't have known about it if he hadn't reported it to us. We spent a lot of time with Dick on that investigation and eventually we prosecuted the case.

One year I was flying caribou surveys and landed at Dick's place because I was really low on fuel. I asked him if he had any aviation fuel because I was afraid I might not even have enough to get back to Port Alsworth. Dick replied, "Well, I've got a five-gallon can that Dave left with me." The fuel had been left several years before but it was in a steel can and it had never been opened. So I put in the five gallons and made it back to Port Alsworth without a problem. We repaid Dick at the first opportunity. The man was always generous.

My entire family got to meet Dick on one of my last visits with him. I owned a T-craft, which I put on floats in the summer and skis or wheels in the winter. One summer my wife was taking care of Jay and Bella Hammond's place on Lake Clark while they were fishing on the Naknek River. Our young daughter Megan was with us and before she went back into Anchorage to get ready for school, she announced: "I'd like to say goodbye to Dick." The next day I flew her up to Twin Lakes and when Dick saw Megan get out of the airplane he said, "Well, if it isn't my favorite rock hound." Megan had this habit of picking up rocks and just treasuring them. Dick had a sharp memory.

After visiting with Dick and hiking up to Teetering Rock we said our final goodbyes and crawled into the T-craft. It was a beautiful day, one of those rare ones when Upper Twin Lake is glassy calm. I had just refueled in Port Alsworth before taking off for the Hammond's, where I picked up Megan and all of her stuff from the summer. I throttled up the T-craft and it climbed up on step but we were still on the water as we approached the connecting stream. I couldn't get off the water. I taxied back to Dick's and left about half of our cargo with him. We finally made it off without a problem but I had to go back later and pick up the rest of Megan's belongings.

In 1977 Paul Haertel transferred to Alaska to become Chief of Operations for the state's five existing national parks and monuments. In late 1978, he became pilot/chief ranger at Lake Clark and eventually its first superintendent. Those were challenging years, when pilots in green and gray uniforms were viewed with suspicion by local residents, including Dick. Paul's humble demeanor and face-to-face contacts with residents spared Lake Clark the controversy that characterized many of the other ANILCA parks.

He was always out, he didn't spend much time in that cabin

Larry Van Slyke

June 16, 1986. Out climbed Larry and from the passenger side a pretty girl. Larry introduced her as Lisa who worked in the Anchorage office. It was going to be another very warm day. We had quite a good visit. RLP

I remember the day I flew over Twin Lakes and could see Dick's snowshoe tracks heading down and across the upper lake. They led down to the isthmus between the upper and lower lakes and then disappeared into the timber by Emerson Creek. With no sign of the man who made the tracks, I landed at Dick's cabin and dropped off his mail and some supplies. A week later I returned, and this time I found him home. While we were talking I said, "I noticed your snowshoe tracks heading down lake last week, have you ever thought about skis? They'd make it a whole lot quicker to get from here to there." Dick paused for a moment and then replied, "Well, when you're by yourself you can't afford to wrench a knee or anything like that when it's thirty below."

I said, "Well, I guess that's the cheechako (Alaska greenhorn) in me, I never thought about it that way. There is a far lower probability of being injured on snowshoes than on skis."

[Authors note: Dick actually made a pair of wooden skis out of spruce. They were over seven feet long and probably used to travel on rotten lake ice in the spring. Based on their condition today, they do not appear to have been used much.]

In 1975 my wife and I took a trip to Alaska and while we were there I bought a book entitled *One Man's Wilderness-An Alaskan Odyssey*. After reading it cover to cover I said to my wife, "You know, before I kick the bucket I'm going to stand under the eaves of that cabin." Four years later in 1979, I had the pleasure of doing just that. My partner and I were dropped off on Upper Twin Lake and we set up camp near

Emerson Creek. As we finished pitching our tent we looked up to see a canoe coming down the lake. Dick Proenneke was an unmistakable sight. We met him at the beach and had an enjoyable hour of conversation.

After inviting us to join him at his cabin the next day he climbed back into his canoe and pushed off for the paddle home. What I have never forgotten is that when he departed there was a strong wind blowing down lake. This meant he had to paddle across and up the lake quartering into a headwind the whole way. He never stopped. As long as I could see him, he never missed a stroke paddling that canoe. My partner and I stood there marveling over what strength and endurance that man had.

Later that year, I sent Dick a Christmas card and I signed it, "The future Chief Ranger of Lake Clark National Park and Preserve." Dick responded with a short Christmas letter in which he asked, "Well, does this mean you got the job?"

That was wishful thinking on my part, because it would be years before I would see Dick's cabin again. I spent the next two years in the Grand Canyon but then returned to Alaska to join a task force of twenty-two Rangers assigned to the 40 million acres of new Park Service land created under the Alaska National Interest Lands Conservation Act (ANILCA).

My area of responsibility included Lake Clark National Park. I had a house in Anchorage during the winter and worked out of an office in the Federal Building. When the weather allowed I would always try to go through Merrill Pass to begin my patrol on the north end of the park. During the six years that followed I really got to know Dick well. Before I flew out into the park I'd always go to the grocery store and buy oranges, apples, and whatever I thought Dick might be interested in having. More often than not whenever I'd land at his cabin in the wintertime he was out snowshoeing somewhere. He didn't spend much time in that cabin.

During the summer my duty station was in Port Alsworth. In 1985 we installed some radio repeaters out in the Park and Preserve so that we could communicate back to the field headquarters from the air or when we were on the ground in base camps. We put a repeater on one of the peaks above Twin Lakes. One day I asked Dick, "Hey, would you be interested in having a portable radio here for communications?" Dick thought for minute and replied, "Oh, I'm not very interested in that."

I said, "Well, the reason I asked is that you're the eyes and ears up here, if you saw somebody poaching a bear or a sheep you could get a hold of us."

That struck a nerve. Dick perked up and said, "Oh, well, ah, I guess maybe that does make sense. "

On my next stop I gave Dick a portable radio. I told him there was no need to take the radio with him when he left the cabin, just use it to call us in the morning and the evening each day. I explained that during the radio calls we could pass along information such as an overdue airplane or a missing hiker. He picked up on the morning and evening radio calls quickly and soon was calling in at other times of the day. I think he sort of enjoyed being able to talk to somebody, especially in the wintertime.

Initially he was reluctant to have this technological link to the outside world, but it turned out to be beneficial for both him and us. As he grew older it was just a little bit of life insurance for him. If he had a serious accident he had a way to get a message to us. Radio communication allowed us to schedule visits and take Dick on aerial patrols or surveys such as radio tracking caribou or counting moose. He was always a big help to the seasonal rangers that were stationed at Twin Lakes during the summer time. He sort of took them under his wing.

The more time I spent with Dick the more I began to appreciate how he was the true ambassador of Twin Lakes. I was always amazed at how many people would come to visit Dick's cabin during the summer months. Every time I was up there it seemed like there was somebody at his cabin. Lake Clark National Park and Preserve would not be what it is without the legacy of Dick Proenneke.

I will never forget the day I was at his cabin with a group of visitors from the Sierra Club. I was talking to a lady while Dick was standing just off to my side telling the rest of the group how he built his cabin. The woman asked me, "So what is it that makes Twin Lakes so

special?" The question caught me flat-footed and I fumbled around for a good answer. Then I remembered Dick's words from the film "*One Man's Wilderness.*" Words that were embedded in my brain from watching it dozens of times. With authority, I regurgitated verbatim what he said in his movie, "What makes Twin Lakes so special is that in other places in Alaska you can find bear, sheep, caribou, and moose if you look far and wide, but Twin Lakes has all of those species."

Dick heard me and turned around with a smile on his face. I think it sort of stunned him that I'd come up with one of his lines from his movie, word for word. It filled the hole in the conversation I was having with this woman. But I was quick to add, "That's not my answer, it belongs to Dick Proenneke, who is standing right here."

My cherished time with Dick ended after I became the Chief Ranger at Zion National Park in Utah. Before I left I asked Hollis Twitchell if he'd take my copy of *One Man's Wilderness* up to Dick to see if he would autograph it for me. Dick signed my book and put a little note in between the pages. It read, "Well, I went back through my journals and wall calendars and saw that you pulled the tail of your floats up on my beach sixty-five times during your years at Lake Clark National Park." But of course that was just the times I visited on floats, I was up at his place a lot in winter when I landed on skis.

Larry Van Slyke retired in 2001 after a career that spanned more than 30 years with the National Park Service. His most treasured years were those in which he pulled his floatplane onto Dick Proenneke's beach.

We saw a small wiry man get out of the grader

Frank and Jeanne Moore

We first saw Dick Proenneke at Port Alsworth. Paul Haertel, the Superintendent of the newly established Lake Clark National Park and Preserve, took us to see and work on the "House on the Point", recently purchased from Al Woodward. He was going to leave Jeanne and me at the house, but first he wanted us to meet all of the Alsworths and Laddie and Glenda Elliot.

We taxied across the bay, went up to the house to meet them all, but I was intrigued watching a fellow that was doing an unbelievable job grading and crowning the runway of the airport. He was truly a master of his equipment. We met all of the locals and then saw a small, wiry man get out of the grader and come toward us, and was introduced to us as THE Dick Proenneke of Twin Lakes. We saw Dick several times after that when he would come down to Port Alsworth for one reason or another.

Then one day Paul flew us up to see the Twin Lakes area and we had the opportunity to be shown by Dick the cabin he had built with hand tools only. It was truly a work of art, not like most of the construction I had seen in that area or anywhere. Amazing!! Jeanne was captivated by the very small entry door and the beautiful, hand crafted latches, hinges and lock, as was I.

Not too much later Jeanne and I went to Lower Twin Lake to make an old shack into living quarters for Park Employees when needed. It was there we spent as much time as possible with Dick, hiking, or by canoe, and was shown much of the area by him, his trails, bear dens, streams, you name it. We had some friends come visit us, Dr. Larry Hall and his wife Roberta, and she found a bear den close to Dick's cabin that he did not know was there. To say he was disturbed was to put it mildly.

One day Jack and Ethyl Ross of Port Alsworth came up to visit us. We were having lunch with Dick where the river enters Lower Twin when they arrived, and, as they brought a great meal with them, we had a real picnic. After a great visit, Dick, Jeanne and I watched Jack taxi down the lake a small distance, turn around and took off toward us and the river mouth. Jack did not gain enough altitude, hit a little ridge alongside the lake, flipped the plane over and crashed. We jumped into Dick's canoe and went across to the crash site, expecting to see them both either dead or severely injured. Jack seemed ok, but Ethyl looked as if she might have a broken back at least.

Dick and I jumped into the canoe and headed down the full length of the Lower Twin Lake into a strong headwind and waves, as fast as possible, never slowing a beat to get to the Park Service Cabin where I had a radio. I called the Park Service on the radio and they, as well as Glen, Babe and Bea (Alsworth) all flew up to help us. Ethyl was taken to Anchorage and the Hospital, and Jack came back to help fix his plane up enough to be flown back to Port Alsworth. Miracle worker with Aircraft, Bea Alsworth, brought in a spare float and made the plane flyable. Jack, Ethyl and the T-Craft all recovered. Later Dick said he was amazed that the he and I could maintain that much speed for that long of a distance in the canoe, and under such trying conditions.

Jeanne and I have some truly great memories of our time shared with Dick and still see him in our minds eye, with that great smile of his breaking out on his face, showing us his country. I have been forever grateful we were in excellent physical condition so we usually could keep up with that small man that was a human dynamo. What a treasure that money could never buy is deposited in our memory BANK. Thank you LORD!!

The Moores say the best thing in their lives has been each other, but the second best has been the people they have befriended. Some were famous, like writer and conservationist Jack Hemingway, the son of Ernest Hemingway, and some were unforgettable, like Dick Proenneke.

There's no worms in these blueberries!

Geraldine Straty

"There are many definitions of living but there is one that I never heard and I think should be added. Living is picking in a patch of very large blueberries after a summer rain. It is one more little detail to make living in the wilderness worthwhile" RLP

When I first flew into Twin Lakes to visit Dick Proenneke at his cabin he served me some blueberries with milk and sugar. He said he had just picked them fresh that morning up on Cowgill Bench. Where I live in southeast Alaska the blueberries always have small worms in them. Before we ate or froze any blueberries we had to soak them in a pot of salt water. That killed the worms and they floated to the surface where I could skim them off.

After Dick handed me a bowl of blueberries and I had thanked him, I said in a soft whisper to my husband, "I don't know if I can eat these, you know, there's worms in the blueberries."

Dick heard me, turned around and said with a stern looking frown, "There's no worms in these blueberries!"

Silence followed as I picked up my spoon, ate the blueberries, and enjoyed them.

Of course Dick was right. I found out when I started to pick them that there were no worms. I was kind of embarrassed that I had made that remark, but Dick was a very gracious host and quickly let it pass.

That's the one thing I really miss, picking blueberries up north. They have a wonderful flavor and I love them. I don't harvest blueberries in Juneau anymore. They just don't have a very good taste. And, not so much the worms cause, you know, you're used to that.

[Editor's note: The "worms" in blueberries in southeast Alaska are the early growth stages of a moth and a sawfly. The eggs are laid in spring and the larvae develop in the berries over the summer. In the

fall, the larvae drop to the ground, pupate, and emerge as adults the next spring.]

In 1979, my husband and I flew over from our cabin at Telaquana Lake to see Dick on our honeymoon. As we were visiting, Dick said that he had a wedding gift for us. I thought, "A wedding gift. How could he get a wedding gift?" And then he came out with this birch soup ladle that he had carved. "Ooh," I thought, "that's pretty special." It's a gorgeous piece of workmanship and incredibly smooth. He must have sanded it for hours. It was really thoughtful of him to do that. I never use it though. It's too pretty.

Geraldine's husband, Dick Straty, built a cabin at Telaquana Lake in the late 1950s and after their marriage in 1979, Geraldine shared his love for the area. Dick Proenneke called Geraldine "Swamp Girl" since she grew up in Louisiana, but Geraldine has lived in the Juneau, Alaska vicinity for over sixty years. Geraldine is known for her blueberry pies. But only made with berries from Twin or Telaquana Lakes, of course.

You can call me Dick

Tom Betts

I met Dick Proenneke in 1982 when I was a seasonal park ranger on my first summer assignment in Alaska. My partner, Tim Wingate, and I would be flown to Twin Lakes for a variety of assignments. We would often be out there for ten days at a time. We'd always check in with Dick whenever we were up there. He was very welcoming, very friendly, and he helped us out with all kinds of things. I was always amazed at his cabin, cache, and woodshed—how immaculate they were, and the craftsmanship they exhibited.

Occasionally I'd be up there on my own. One such occasion was when Tim had to unexpectedly fly to the coast to work on a bear poaching case. When I arrived at Twin Lakes the weather was terrible, a strong east wind and rain. I walked over to Dick's cabin and he invited me in for dinner. I seem to recall that we had fish. But what I'll never forget is the salad. He made a fireweed, smoked salmon salad that was just out of this world. I couldn't believe I was eating this well out in the bush. After dinner he took me up lake to one of the other cabins where I spent the night.

Tim and I went on numerous hikes with Dick and quickly learned that he could hike like no one we had ever met. Dick was in his late sixties and we were in our early twenties, but on more than one occasion he would kick our butts. We were just young sprouts and we should have been able to keep right up with him. He would hike from Twin Lakes to the head of Lake Clark, catch a ride across the lake, and walk down to Port Alsworth. He was an amazing outdoorsman.

He kept a daily journal, and I'm afraid that on some days I made the headlines with all the stupid things I did while I was up there. Like the time I was there by myself on a stakeout for illegal hunting activity. Dick invited me to stay with him one night while I was on his side of the lake. As it was getting dark I heard an airplane and stepped outside to see that it was flying down from the head of the Upper Lake, a direction that planes didn't usually originate when the weather was bad. It landed at a cabin across the lake.

I had been warned earlier about that cabin. It was suspected of being used for illegal hunting activities. The next morning I loaded some gear into a Klepper kayak and paddled over there. I saw where the hunters had beached the plane, but both the plane and a boat that I'd seen at the cabin the previous night were gone.

I secured the kayak on the beach and did a long scouting hike on the slope behind the cabin, looking for any sign of poaching. There were several Dall sheep on a ridge, but I couldn't find anything suspicious. At one point, I was almost run over by a big bull moose. As I was walking back toward the kayak, I heard some pounding coming from a cabin at the east end of the lake. That seemed peculiar so I launched the kayak and paddled to that end of the lake.

I parked the boat where it couldn't be seen and walked up the cabin. As I got close I saw three or four men wandering around. As I watched they all entered the cabin. They hadn't seen me yet. And so, using good Alaska etiquette, I yelled out, "Hello, in the cabin."

As there was no response, I stepped out of the tall brush into the open and immediately saw the head of a Dall sheep ram lying next to the cabin. I knew it was an illegal take. Then the door of the cabin opened and out walked four guys with rifles. I immediately jumped back into the brush and retraced my steps to the kayak, jumped in and started paddling away from there as fast as I could. I didn't know what was going to happen next, but I looked back a couple of times and saw all four on the beach, watching me. I just kept going and going until finally I was within a mile or so of Dick's cabin. About that time, by some miraculous coincidence, our Park Service airplane flew over with rangers Hollis Twitchell and Mike Tollefson on board.

I had dropped my aircraft radio in the water earlier that week and Dick had been kind enough to let me dry it out in his cabin. It worked when I'd tested it that morning but if I ever needed it to work it was now. I hailed Hollis and Mike on the radio and let them know what I'd seen. They turned around and said they would land in front of Dick's cabin and wait for me. I picked up the pace, paddling like a fiend, trying to get down the lake because I didn't know what was going on behind me. Whether they even recognized me as a National Park Service Ranger or whether I was going to get shot in the back.

Finally I rounded Carrithers's Point and saw Dick, Hollis, and Mike standing next to the Park floatplane. As I reached shore I looked up to see Dick smiling. I felt foolish, having gone after those poachers like that. Then something happened to make me feel even worse. I had one of those brand new breakfront holsters for my handgun. Apparently I hadn't secured it very well, because as I hastily exited the kayak the gun hooked on the boat, flipped out backwards, and dropped into the lake. Right in front of Dick and my supervisor.

I was lucky. The water was shallow and I was able to reach down and retrieve my handgun. It was a totally embarrassing moment, especially in front of Dick, who would never have made such a clumsy mistake.

The three of us immediately flew up to the head of lake. Fortunately no one had left the cabin. We contacted the individuals, issued them a citation for an illegal take, and confiscated the ram. In hindsight, after all the humorous mistakes, I did a couple of things right. In the end my actions helped us catch an illegal hunting party within the newly created Park and Dick was always passionate about nailing poachers.

I wish that I could say that was my only embarrassing moment that summer. One day we were dropped off at Twin Lakes with the Klepper kayak. Earlier that day we had hastily loaded everything into the floatplane at Port Alsworth. After we had the kayak assembled on the beach and our gear loaded in the boat we realized that we'd forgotten the paddles.

So here we were in a Klepper kayak with no paddles on the opposite side of the lake from Dick Proenneke. With no other option we asked ourselves, "What would Dick do?" Our solution was to walk up and down the beach looking for driftwood that resembled a paddle. We found two decent pieces and paddled off. Thankfully, the wind was not blowing. Dick was home and he was kind enough to lend us a real paddle, a double-ender. So I ended up paddling in the rear while Tim sat up front. Two days later the park plane arrived and when pilot-ranger Tollefson stepped out onto the floats he asked, "Did you forget something?"

* * *

One thing I found out about Dick that sticks with me to this day is that you should treat everybody with respect. Perhaps that's because it coincides with my own upbringing. When you first meet someone you should address them by title, not just their first name. When I and my partner first met Dick, he was very respectful, friendly, helpful, and very interested in what we were doing. During those initial visits I greeted Dick as Mr. Proenneke. But after a couple of meetings he said, "You can call me Dick."

One day I learned that Dick did have a sharp side to his personality. The early 1980s must have been anxious times for Dick and many others that lived inside the boundaries of newly created parks and preserves. His cabin was illegal at the time, but of course we gave him five-year leases and ultimately a lifetime lease. But it's under-standable that Dick was apprehensive whenever high-ranking Park officials came to his cabin.

That year two Associate Regional Park Service Directors flew in to meet Dick. High level Park administrators, although well-intentioned, can sometimes seem a bit arrogant. Maybe it rubs off on them during their stints in Washington, like spruce pollen on a moose.

I was at Dick's place the day the Associate Directors visited. They spent about half an hour meeting with him but I wasn't involved. After they left I asked Dick, "So, how'd your visit go?" He instantly lit into them. He said, "Well, they got off that airplane, introduced themselves as Director this and Director that, and then called me by my first name like we went to school together."

It offended him that these Park Service directors wanted respect be-cause of their lofty titles, yet they didn't extend the same level of es-teem to him. For me, this event was quite a good lesson in etiquette and the importance of treating everybody with utmost regard.

As I grew to know him and learn of his many talents and accomplishments, I developed a great admiration for the man. To this day, I remain in awe of everything he did and stood for.

Being a park ranger comes naturally for Tom Betts – you could say it's in his blood. He is the son of a park ranger. After racing to stay behind Dick Proenneke on those hikes at Twin Lakes, Tom never slowed down. He moved on to become chief ranger at many of the crown jewels of the National Park System, including Wrangell-St Elias and Bandelier. He was the 2013 recipient of the Harry Yount Award, the most prestigious national honor given to a park ranger. Tom is currently chief ranger at Katmai National Park and Preserve.

I want to take you up my mountain

Mrs. Frank (Kathy) Betts

August 10, I put a fresh pot of Navy beans to soak and while the beans bubbled I was writing a letter to Frank and Kathy Betts at Ft. Collins, Colorado. Kathy was here and kayaked on the lakes with her good friend Susie Tollefson. It was they who gave me my first guest book. I reported that it is near filled. RLP

My husband Frank (Betts) was superintendent of Mount McKinley (now Denali) National Park from 1978 to 1980. He owned a Cessna 182 aircraft and one summer a few years later he flew my friend Susie (Tollefson) and me down to Lake Clark National Park. My son Tom had spent a year there as a seasonal park ranger and had such wonderful tales of his time at Twin Lakes with Dick Proenneke that I wanted to see it for myself. We were going to float down one of the rivers in the area with our kayak, but the water levels were pretty low that year so we opted instead to go into Twin Lakes.

We were dropped off on the east end of the Lower Lake below the connecting stream. We spent the first night there and then the next morning we portaged to the Upper Lake and slowly made our way toward Hope Creek delta where my son had told me Dick lived. It was late and raining when we arrived at Hope Creek so we just unloaded and set up our tent.

We didn't report that we were there but Dick had gotten the news that two girls were down the road from him. The next morning we were sitting on the beach when a man came paddling by in his canoe. I'd never seen Dick before and had no idea whether he was short or tall or what he looked like. I tried to remember what Tom told me about his appearance. As he got closer I turned to Susie and said, "Well, that's got to be Dick." And it was. He'd been out fishing and he invited us to dinner. Dick must have gotten the word from one of the pilots that we were there because he had no other way of getting messages. No emails and no telephone.

That afternoon we went out and explored the upper end of the lake. We fought a headwind and a steady rain all the way up the lake but we were determined to get there. We thought at least we'd have a fast trip home. But when we got to the head of the lake the wind quit. The view was incredible and well worth the paddle. We could have stayed longer but we were anxious to get back and have dinner with Dick. It had been an incredible day, and that evening Dick was a lot of fun. For dinner he took a couple fish fillets and cut them into small two-inch squares, rolled them in flour and cayenne pepper, and then fried them. Then he prepared fireweed salad and sourdough pancakes to go with the trout. Both the meal and the preparation were fantastic.

After dinner Dick said, "Ok now, tomorrow, I want to take you up my mountain." When we arrived at his cabin the next morning he gave us each a walking stick from a collection that he kept by his woodshed. Then he slung a big [spotting] scope over his shoulder. It was huge. We started up a path that paralleled Hope Creek for a while and then ascended onto open tundra. Along the way Dick said, "I come up here and then I can see what critters have come out." He told us how he kept records in his journal of the first day he observed this or that animal. He also pointed out the flowers along the trail and identified the birds we heard calling.

As we made our way along the side of Crag Mountain we crossed over to what Dick called, "the knoll of a dozen spruce." The view of the lake was incredible there so we stopped and ate our lunch. It was fun to hear him talk about his life up there and how long he'd been doing this. He was just a special guy. Then we headed back down by way of Split Rock and Teetering Rock. Dick seemed to have a name for every stop along the way. Dick told us about Teetering Rock and then told Suzy to watch and count how many times it moved. Suzy counted twenty-four movements after Dick had tilted it to the limit and set it free to rock.

Dick walked over to our campsite the next morning when our floatplane arrived to pick us up. We both thanked him and gave him a big hug. We told him how much we enjoyed Twin Lakes and said we would like to come again and make that circle around Cowgill

Mountain that he told us about. I have one enduring memory of that trip; I'm still using his sourdough starter. I've kept it going all these years.

We took a number of photographs of Dick, his cabin, and our hikes and paddles at Twin Lakes. Of course they were taken with a real camera, not a phone. The day before we left Twin Lakes we asked Dick if he had a guest book for people to sign. He replied, "No, I never have." When Susie and I got back to Anchorage, we went to a shop and bought a nice guest book. It had a wooden cover and a place on the front where you could insert a photograph. We put our favorite picture of his cabin on the cover, signed the book, and mailed it to him. I don't know who has that book now or what they did with it but I'm sure he had lots of folks sign it after that.

Kathy Betts owes her memorable days with Dick Proenneke to her son Tom and low water levels in the rivers. But Lake Clark was only one of many parks she would spend time in. Along with her husband, Frank, they spent twenty years presenting financial workshops to the employees of the National Park Service. These allowed them to experience visiting over sixty National Park units.

It should be about 155 canoe strokes to the cabin

Andy Hutchison

September 7. A strong wind in the spruce all night and rain drops thudding on the moss roof at daylight. Rain spilling over the high peaks as it was getting light down country. The lake was wild, there would be no crossing it today. RLP

I first met Dick Proenneke in June of 1987. Chief Park Ranger Larry Van Slyke flew me to Upper Twin Lake and dropped me off at his cabin. After a brief welcome Larry took off and Dick and I put his canoe in the water and paddled up the lake. Along the way Dick pointed out the various cabins and hunting sites from which he salvaged a lot of moose meat.

We spent a couple of hours near the head of the lake and were heading back towards his cabin when Dick asked, "Andy, you are from back east. Can you help me with a problem?" He said, "I've got some money to invest. Should I stay in common stock or invest it all in a mutual fund?"

"Dick," I said, "I don't know a darn thing about finances or investments but I'll ask my wife."

We canoed on for another hour or so when Dick said, "Let's go get some lunch. It should be about 155 canoe strokes to the cabin." It took us 161. Lunch was Dick's special sourdough flapjacks rolled and filled with peanut butter and jelly. This was his mainstay, and a few were always in his pack.

Later that year I was staying at the park's ranger cabin on the west end of Lower Twin Lake. Early one morning the wind picked up blowing down lake. Big whitecaps started pounding the beach and heavy rain began to fall. Dick called me on the radio to tell me not to go out and asked if everything was okay. I told him I was concerned about the Zodiac raft being tossed on the rocks. Dick replied: "I'll see you in a little over an hour."

Sure enough, as I was looking out the window I saw Dick walking up the beach toward the raft. He told me to get the motor off and find some big rocks. I did both those things, selecting rocks that weighed about forty pounds each. Dick pulled up his boots and waded into the lake. He found a place just off shore with a good sandy bottom then he brought the raft over and placed the rocks in it. He maneuvered it to the selected spot, pulled the plug and the Zodiac collapsed on a soft cushion of sand.

The weather continued to deteriorate and I encouraged him to spend the night. He said, "No. I've got to go home. I'll see you in the morning."

When he returned the next day we pumped the boat up and it was good as ever.

Every year the seasonal staff at Lake Clark seemed to include at least two women. For some reason, each of them wanted to be stationed at Twin Lakes. They all considered Dick a true disciple of the environmental movement. Because of Dick's book and the TV coverage of him, they all knew of him before they arrived at Port Alsworth.

To me Dick was an outstanding craftsman. His building skills were beyond comparison. He was a superb woodsman and a keen observer of wildlife. He was truly independent and self-sufficient. Dick had a gentle personality and I never heard him make a negative remark about anyone.

To the seasonal staff he was a couple of steps above this. They compared him to Thoreau, and Twin Lakes to Walden Pond.

One day one of these seasonal employees returned from her days off during which she had gone to Anchorage. She brought Dick a large box of green vegetables and proceeded to give Dick a lecture about his diet. In particular, she was very critical of his consumption of bacon. Next she said he ought to cut down on the peanut butter.

She went through the box of vegetables, pointing out the lettuce, spinach and celery. Dick said thanks and told her to bring a bigger box next time so he could store it in his cache till Thanksgiving. Then

Dick turned to me and said, "Andy, go catch us three fish for lunch." This was not much of a challenge in Hope Creek at that time. Dick dressed the three trout and stirred the fried potatoes on the stove. Next, he set the table and put a plate aside for the greens. He directed the seasonal worker to put some greens on each plate. She made an attractive salad with spinach, lettuce and scallions. Dick put a trout on each plate along with some of his homemade fries. But before he sat down to eat he took the grease and leavings in the frying pan and dripped it over the salad. There were no more comments on his diet!

One summer's day in 1991 Dick called me and asked me to come up for a little party. When I got to Dick's cabin he introduced me to two middle-aged women. They were both well dressed and very cordial. I don't recall their names but one of the women was a descendant of Adolph Murie, the early naturalist at Mt. McKinley. They were there to celebrate Dick's 75th birthday. One of the ladies was from Providence, Rhode Island. I believe she was the person to give Dick a subscription to the Sunday edition of the New York Times. It always arrived over a week late but Dick read it in its entirety.

Dick asked the lady from Rhode Island about the state motto "Hope." He said it seemed a little weak to him compared to "Liberty or Death." This triggered an instant response from her. She told Dick about the religious prejudice of the Massachusetts Bay Colony. She went on to tell Dick about Roger Williams and Anne Hutchinson in their search for a safe haven. Then she gave Dick a short lesson in basic grammar and word usage – pointing out that "Hope" could be either a noun or a verb. To her, "Hope" was surely a noun. The other lady, sensing things were going downhill, insisted that we have cake and a glass of wine. Dick had a small piece of cake but refused the wine. I sensed that after they left Dick would have an even greater appreciation for being in the wilderness of Twin Lakes, thousands of miles from Rhode Island.

Dick was a complex character. Whenever I asked him about his time in Iowa and his Naval Service during World War II, he did not respond. To me Dick was sort of an enigma; he was easy to understand but difficult to figure out.

Andy Hutchinson was Superintendent of Lake Clark National Park and Preserve from 1987-1992. In addition to his admiration for Dick Proenneke, he had a deep love for the Park, its wildlife, and especially its fish.

I would like you to take over when we come to the stage three rapids

Clair Roberts

July 24. Today was meant for canoe travel. I would go to the lower end of the lower lake where the Chilikadrotna River begins its long swift journey to merge with the Mulchatna and Nushagak. RLP

Early one summer, Park Ranger Maggie Yurrick and I were assigned to float the Chilikadrotna River (Chili) to map and record campsites within the boundary of the Park and Preserve. We asked Dick Proenneke if he would like to come along. Initially he said no. When we asked again, he agreed, but only under the condition that we would pick up trash along the river, including any outside the park boundaries.

I was not surprised at Dick's request. From the time he first arrived at Twin Lakes Dick had been patrolling the shorelines and picking up trash discarded by others. I'm sure he had seen trash along the Chili River during his hikes out toward the Bonanza Hills. On foot there was little he could do about it, but this trip would be the perfect opportunity to remove it.

The Chili is a National Wild and Scenic River that extends sixty miles from Lower Twin Lake to its confluence with the Mulchatna River. We began our expedition at the mouth of the river and intended to float its entire length. Dick joined us just as we finished pumping up the five-man raft, which would carry us to our take out point. We anticipated that the trip would last three or four days. Unlike today, the Chili was seldom floated in the 1980s. Depending upon the water level, there is only one major set of white-water rapids, a Class III. The only real concern is the sweepers (fallen trees extending across the river).

We entered the mouth of the river and found the first dozen miles easy going. There were many large rocks but they were easy to dodge. We stopped often to look for campsites and gas cans that I had seen from the air. After the first couple of miles Maggie took over the oars and Dick and I walked the banks looking for trash.

We took a break when we were next to Trail Butte and Dick told us about the wolf dens he knew of in that area. He also showed us the spot where he had filmed a group of fifty-eight caribou bulls, footage that appeared in the movie *One Man's Alaska*.

We floated late, looking for a good place to spend the night. Up to this point progress seemed slow, but after leaving the Preserve we no longer inventoried campsites and just focused on picking up raft debris and garbage from the river. The vast majority of what we found was rusty, discarded five-gallon fuel cans. They were quite old and Dick said they were likely left by winter caribou hunters. We also found the remains of a wrecked Klepper kayak and even a tire, but not much in the way of cans and bottles.

All three of us shared the rowing. Dick seemed like an old hand at the oars. Eventually he told us that he had a lot of experience rowing boats on Kodiak Island. Late in the third day we encountered lots of rocks and some fast water. When the river settled down Dick said, "Clair, I would like you to take over when we come to the stage three rapids." After the next stop I took over and we remained alert, watching and waiting for the rapids. At the end of the day I checked our position on the map and found that we had run the rapids that morning while Dick was at the oars! That news put a smile on Dick's face; I think he felt pretty confident that he could handle anything after that.

We did pretty well until late in the trip when we approached our pullout. The river braids a lot at that point and we picked the wrong channel. Just around the corner we slammed into a tree that had fallen completely across the river. It didn't hurt the raft, but we had to use a hatchet and bow saw to chop and cut our way out of that one.

I remember we ate a lot fish and blueberries on that trip. We saw some king salmon but never caught one. We passed Dummy Creek on the fourth morning and a mile below was our pick up point, a long smooth section of the river. Bee Alsworth picked us up a few hours later in his brother Glen's Beaver.

* * *

Everyone who ever worked at the park knew of Dick Proenneke. He was a local legend, widely known for his wilderness ethics, self-reliance and craftsmanship, as well as his published book and self-made films. It was during our first initial park orientation that I first learned about Dick, but it was later in the summer of 1981 that we met.

After I became a permanent employee I spent a good deal of time with Dick, accompanying him on many of his favorite hikes such as those to Teetering Rock and eye of the needle. And of course there was our float with him on the Chilikadrotna River. Many years later when Dick "retired" to California to live with his brother Raymond, my wife, Liz, and I would visit him in Hemet. In his final years, Dick walked the neighborhood on a regular basis and cleaned up the litter on his beat; just like he did for thirty years at Twin Lakes. We miss him.

Clair Roberts was one of the first seasonal Park Rangers at Lake Clark National Park and Preserve, working three summers and winters from 1981 to 1983. He returned for a second tour as a permanent Park Ranger for several more years in the 1990s.

Dick poses in front of his cabin. *Photo courtesy of R. Proenneke.*

On snowshoes mid-way up Hope Creek Valley with the base of "Proenneke Peak" visible over Dicks left shoulder. *Photo courtesy of R. Proenneke.*

Photographing wildlife with the Bolex camera above Hope Creek
on Cowgill Mountain. *Photo courtesy of R. Proenneke.*

Hiking up the east side of Hope Creek Valley in early fall.
LACL1978JK_2220508

Admiring the glaciers to the right and left of a peak up the east valley at the head of Upper Twin Lake. *LACL1969RLP_0110617*

Laurel asks Dick a question as he looks south from Low Pass toward Big Valley.

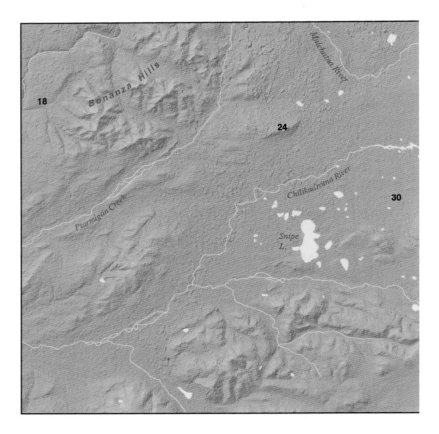

Map Key
1. Allen Mt.
2. Beech Creek
3. Bell Mt.
4. Big Valley
5. Blueberry Hill
6. Carrithers's Point
7. Connecting Stream
8. Cowgill Benches
9. Cowgill Peak
10. Crag Mt

11. Dick's Cabin
12. Emerson Creek
13. Eye of the
        Needle
14. Falls Creek
15. Falls Mt.
16. First Canyon
17. Frank Bell's Cabin
18. Gill's Camp
19. Glacier Creek

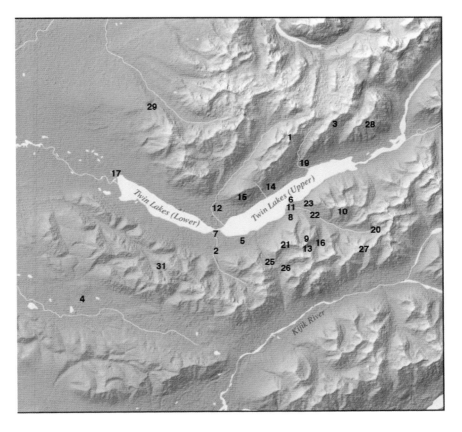

20. Graveyard of the Stones
21. Gold Mt.
22. Hope Creek
23. The Hump
24. Island Mt.
25. Low Pass
26. Low Pass Basin
27. Proenneke Peak
28. Rockpile Mt.
29. Sheep Lick
23. Split Rock
23. Teetering
      Rock
30. Trail Butte
31. Volcanic Mts

Dick looks down on Emerson Creek from the top of Falls Mountain in late March.

Checking out a brown bear den on the slopes across the lake from his cabin. *Photo courtesy of National Park Service*

Standing next to his beloved Teetering Rock. *Photo courtesy of Rick Phillips*

With John Denver (left) and bush pilot Stu Ramstad. *Photo courtesy of Rick Phillips*

Dick Weisser positioning the ridge log on his cabin at Upper Twin Lakes while Dick and Raymond Proenneke were up the lake cutting the spruce pole rafters. *Photo courtesy of Randy Weisser*

Dick Proenneke handling the oars on a float trip down the Chilikadrotna River. Park Ranger Maggie Yurrick is seated in the stern. *Photo courtesy of Clair Roberts*

Happy Birthday Dick

Patty Brown

July 30, Partly Cloudy, Breeze dn. 43°. Five days of down lake wind and I could hear it out in the stretch during the night. Morning came soon enough and this would be a full day. Pat and party would come up but I didn't expect them early even if we had a long hike ahead of us. Taters for breakfast and I got everything in good order. I would like to dismantle my bear alarm system for I haven't seen any recent sign of bear but I would leave it for another day or two. RLP

In 1991, the National Park Service distributed shiny gold square pins acknowledging its 75th anniversary to all the staff including Dick, the most valuable volunteer in Lake Clark history. I learned that Dick was "only" 73 that year, so I filed that information for future reference. The year he turned 75, I worked at the Kenai National Wildlife Refuge. How could I surprise Dick? Even though he had remained a staunch bachelor his entire life, I knew he still, well, noticed things.

I still had possession of a friend's "Barbie" dress. She had loaned it to me from her collection of formal attire required in association with her employment as an engineer with British Petroleum. Yeah, go figure. I borrowed it initially for sort of a "middle-aged debutante" event on my 36th birthday. It was one of those dresses that stays up despite "no visible means of support." Barbie holds her dresses up with a plastic anatomy. Being squishier, I needed the built-in hardware.

After a flight on Lake Clark Air, I arranged to fly in from Port Alsworth with Leon on the NPS plane and he came with Richard Jones. Richard and I had been counterparts in 1990 and 1991, he at Telaquana, me at Twin, but he had continued to work as a backcountry ranger after I left. I wore my river sandals; I just didn't think I could navigate the rocky beaches even for a few steps if I tried to wear heels. Since Dick only knew me in NPS green and gray, the effect would be enough.

As I stepped out of the plane, Dick walked toward it and almost stumbled in disbelief. I gave him a hug and said, "Happy Birthday, Dick!"

Later Dick decided to reward my effort by digging up a bottle of wine that someone had given him years earlier. He did not normally drink, but thought this unusual event was worth celebrating. We sat on the beach, both of us wearing the more traditional backcountry attire, and popped the bottle open. Dick poured just a little in each cup and we "clinked" then took a sip. Immediately we both spat it out! Turns out he had not followed wine storage recommendations and it had turned to vinegar. It was good for a laugh anyway.

Most mornings, Dick and I would check in with each other on the radio.

"Lower Lake, Upper Lake."

"Upper Lake, Lower Lake."

"What are ya gonna do today?"

"Well, maybe take the Klepper kayak over to the other side and see if berries are ripe. What are you doing?"

"I'm cooking beans."

"OK. Give you a berry update later."

Dick never changed his clock for daylight savings time and thought it was dumb when Alaska merged all its time zones. So his clock was behind mine. If we checked in at 10 A.M., it was only 8 A.M. for him.

Dick utilized the cabins a few hundred yards from his as storage, once it was clear the owners were not coming back. He had scores of fans from all over the U.S. and beyond. One of his admirers didn't live too far away and, in fact, owned the small lodge that had been built in the only private non-native inholding in the Twin Lakes area. Chris Degernes made Dick chocolate peanut clusters a few times a year. Afraid he didn't have the discipline to keep from eating the whole box at once, he stored them at Hope's cabin. Once in a while, on a visit, we would walk down and each get two…one for eating right now and one to take back. His smile was always one of childlike joy, like we were getting away with something.

I always imagined that Dick's overall health, especially his digestive system, was in good shape. He ate oatmeal two times almost every day. That has to be good for the colon. Once was for breakfast and once was for dessert after dinner, "cold porridge pudding," he called it. Sure, he added sugar, plus cinnamon and powdered milk, but it was still mostly oatmeal.

On a hike to Emerson Creek falls, Dick and I were sitting, enjoying the powerful roar. He asked me, "What do you think would happen to someone if they fell in? Do you think they could survive?" We launched into a somewhat macabre conversation about what the injuries might be, what water level would be more forgiving, and more.

One sunny day, Dick and I were relaxing on his well-raked beach enjoying a little chat. I took off my boots and Dick noticed how callused the balls of my feet were there at the base of the big toe, especially. Something about the callusing there caused a really tender place just below it and I was rubbing that spot.

"You need to do something about that, Pat," Dick told me. "You have to take care of your feet."

"What should I do?"

"Lemme see," Dick replied. Off he went to his tool shed and back he came with a fine wood file. As I leaned back on my elbows, knees bent, he took first one foot, then the other and began to rub off the calluses, gently but persistently.

I remarked, "None of my other friends would do this for me."
Dick responded with a twinkle, "Then you need better friends."

Both of the summers I worked at Twin Lakes were marked by heartbreak. In May of 1990, while I was out on the Matanuska River going through Swiftwater Rescue training, a friend was killed by electrocution. It was a freak accident involving some thaw wires along a bike trail that had not been shut off and were in contact with water. She was a new friend; I had known her for three years since we both worked at Glacier Bay, but was a soul sister. It helped me greatly to work through the grief that summer, knowing Dick had known her as well. She worked in Lake Clark, exploring all over in one of the early years after it had become one of the new ANILCA parks. I told Dick one day that I thought I had seen her spirit in the eyes of a red fox I watched at her den near the lower lake cabin, guarding her pups. He nodded and had tears, just as I did.

The second year a relationship of mine that had been on-again, off-again for ten years, was off for good. I had received a "Dear John" letter that ended with "have a nice life." I told Dick about it one afternoon and he posed one question. "Would he have risked his life to save yours?"

I thought about it and said, "I'm not really sure."

Dick was decisive. "Then forget him."

Without Dick's guidance, I know I wouldn't have developed the confidence I needed to be independent and carry out the roles expected in the backcountry. One aspect, in particular, was navigating the connecting stream. If I paddled up lower lake in the kayak, I needed to walk the south shoreline and tow the boat up using two lines to control it in the current. If I used the Zodiac with the outboard, I had to be extremely attentive and follow the exact channel.

One very handy tip Dick passed on to me was using day old sourdough pancakes as sandwich "bread" for hikes. Turns out that rubbery consistency added much durability increasing the appeal of a peanut butter sandwich midway through a hike.

In March of 1991, I decided I had to see Twin Lakes during the season of snow and ice. I was given permission to stay in the ranger cabin and chartered in on a plane with skis. The day I skied up to see Dick was a low light day. I was in pretty good shape and got up there quickly. Coming back was the challenge. I was not that savvy about wilderness skiing on frozen lakes and got too close to the inlet of a stream and fell in nearly to my waist. With a struggle I got out, sprawling out onto the ice closer to mid-lake to distribute my weight. My pants were instantly encased in ice in the cold air. I had about a mile to get to the cabin and I raced against darkness. After I had a fire going, changed into dry clothes, and calmed myself, I called Dick. He had been a little worried about me and said, "Guess you know about thin ice at inlets now!"

On my last visit with Dick he asked me to sign his guest book. Pen in hand I struggled to put my thoughts into words. I wrote: "The tears are in my eyes, just out of sight, and I try to believe it's the wind or the autumn cold, but it's not --- It's my impending departure from Magical Twin Lakes - the best home I've known in years, maybe ever!! I want to come back again, especially in winter to see the place all dressed in white, little foot prints, big icicles and you. Thanks for canoeing, for cold porridge pudding, sourdough biscuits, and all that wilderness news. You are in my heart always!" Patty Brown Lake Clark Ranger

Patty Brown spent twenty years working as a park ranger in Alaska and California, including 1990 and 1991 at Lower Twin Lake. She went on to spend another twenty years teaching science, math and other subjects in Alaska school systems. She is involved in a statewide dialogue to improve education in science, technology, engineering and math.

Rhino

Chris Degernes

I had a male golden retriever named Orion that accompanied my former husband and me on all of our hikes and snowshoe adventures with Dick Proenneke. On one winter snowshoe, Orion scored big points with Dick when he dropped a mitten on a steep icy slope high above Hope Creek. As the mitten slid down the side of the mountain, Orion did what retrievers do—he bounded down the slope and brought it back to Dick.

For some reason Dick thought Orion's name was "Rhino." I couldn't figure out why until one year it occurred to me that every time we went to Dick's place, we'd have to tell Orion not to pee on the sides of the neatly shoveled walkways. As we approached Dick's cabin I'd yell, "Orion, NO!" Dick's hearing had declined with age, and what he thought he heard was RHI-NO. We just let it pass, and over time Orion became "Rhino" to everyone until the day he died.

I first met Dick in February 1987 when my husband and I bought a small parcel of land across the lake from Dick that had been owned by Erv Terry. Dick took a special liking to me over the years and showed me many of his favorite hikes and routes in the Upper Twin Lakes wilderness. I hiked, snowshoed, and paddled hundreds of miles with him over the years. Later, when I was no longer at Twin Lakes, we exchanged many letters and I always marveled at how much he had to say about what he and the animals were doing.

Because I didn't have anything to report from my routine day job that Dick might find interesting, I reported on ecological discoveries that I made on the Kenai Peninsula. I told him about an emaciated juvenile wolverine carcass I found while hiking in the Kenai Mountains; the black bear family that finally found the buried salmon carcasses in my garden after years of burying them; and the strange deformed Dall sheep pelvis that had a huge bone growth on it.

Dick's curiosity about the natural world was fascinating to me. I recall him endlessly pondering how much his Teetering Rock weighed, even going so far as to measure it, calculate its volume in cubic feet, and estimate its weight using published weights for granite. One winter he and I studied some mysterious suspended bubbles in the ice near the connecting stream. Dick's asked, "How did they form? Why didn't they just float to the surface? Why are they so perfectly round and suspended in a uniform pattern?"

He knew his animal neighbors better than many people know some of their suburban human neighbors. I doubt that a brown bear ever denned up on the mountains across from Dick's cabin without him noting the date it went into the den and when it came out the following spring. The number of Dall sheep lambs was always a reportable bit of news that I enjoyed, and of course, our shared dislike for porcupines (or the damage they caused) was a common topic of conversation. Dick made more than a few porkies "farmers," as he liked to say (dead and buried, ready to fertilize whatever plant needed a bit of extra nutrients!).

One day in February, 1987 Dick led me on an epic hike. At least it was epic for me; for Dick it was just another day hike. He called it "around the mountain and through the eye of the needle." We left early one morning, carrying our snowshoes and walking down the lake to Low Pass. Leaving the lake, we put on our snowshoes for the hike up and over Low Pass. On the way, Dick led us across a very steep, rocky talus slope where caribou had pounded out a decent trail from a millennia of use— it would have been tricky and dangerous to cross that steep slope without that caribou trail.

Once we were through the pass, we turned east into an upper side valley and walked to the head of this short valley. We encountered a steep mountainside covered with a stable snowpack and there we took off our snowshoes to boot-step up the steep mountain. I was glad the snow was stable, as this would have been a dangerous avalanche spot otherwise. Dick figured it was safe since it hadn't snowed in a while and things were pretty settled.

Once we reached the ridge top, Dick led us though the eye of the needle, a hole through an archway of rocks, leading from one side of the ridge to the other. I wouldn't have known the opening was there had Dick not lead us to and through it. After briefly pausing on the ridge, we dropped down a steep slope into First Canyon, as Dick called it. At first, the snow was hard packed, making it difficult to get an edge with our boots. Dick had an extra pair of instep crampons he loaned me for the sketchy hike down this steep slope. Rhino had a great time racing up and down that slope. Once we reached the bottom of the canyon it was an easy hike out to Hope Creek and back to Dick's cabin.

Our travel down the side of Hope Creek was mostly done without snowshoes because the western slopes in that area had been heavily windblown that winter. We had to put our snowshoes on for the lower drainage, where we again encountered deep snow. We enjoyed seeing the tracks of wolves, wolverine and fox, "the locals" as Dick called them, plus the numerous ptarmigan that we flushed. The light was beginning to fade when we arrived back at Dick's cabin, and it had been five hours since we left to go "around the mountain."

Dick was a walking encyclopedia of everything Twin Lakes. He knew the history of every cabin, and knew most of the original builders, knew about every plane crash in the area, knew every game trail that would allow him to easily navigate through some of the brushy hillsides around Twin Lakes.

I've never known a person who could put as many miles on his legs as easily as Dick. He commonly walked the legs off people half his age, even as he approached his eightieth birthday. On one hike up and over Low Pass to the Kijik side with a 79-year-old Dick and my sister, we returned after a full and tiring day of exploring to soak our feet in the lake in front of Dick's cabin and eat his famous blueberries with Tang. After a moment he asked: "Well girls, where are we going to hike tomorrow?"

One year I thought Dick might like some new mugs for his cabin because his were chipped and old. He thankfully accepted them but on future visits I never saw them in use. He continued to serve me tea in the old white china mugs. After a few years he handed me the box of mugs I gave him saying "Why don't you take these to your cabin. They'll fit in better over there." He didn't want to hurt my feelings, but he didn't need new mugs because his were fine just the way they were!

"Why buy a tool when you can make your own," he'd say. If Dick needed a plank he'd get out his ripping saw and make one. If he needed a rodent-proof storage bin, he'd cut the top off a discarded tin aviation fuel can, crimp the corners, and slip the top back on for a lid.

On my last visit to see Dick in the late 1990s, he wanted to show some visitors the Teetering Rock above Hope Creek. By then he was pretty frail but still able to make his way up the trail to his favorite rock. He spent time with the visitors from California but it was clear they wanted to keep moving, so they quickly left to make their way down the mountain and back to their boat. It occurred to me that they had just missed out on one of the most unique moments of their lives— to spend some quality time with Dick. If they had only slowed down to savor the moment. But they were still on California time, rushing about and trying to see and do everything they could.

In contrast, I couldn't seem to get enough of visiting with Dick that one last time we were together. I knew when I flew out that I might not see him again, and that turned out to be the case. We continued to exchange letters for a few more years, even as Dick's health failed more and more. His letters are some of my most cherished possessions – words of wisdom from a man I loved and admired.

Although it's been years since Dick's passing, I still think of him whenever I see something unique or interesting in the natural world. How I wish I could tell him about it in a letter and seek his thoughts.

For many years Chris Degernes was Dick Proenneke's nearest neighbor at Twin Lakes. In earlier years her cabin site near the mouth of Falls Creek was intermittently occupied by hunting guides and trappers that Dick writes about in his journals. Today Chris lives at Cooper Landing on the Kenai Peninsula where she watches the seasons change, sharpens her knowledge of the natural world, and occasionally re-reads one of her letters from Dick Proenneke.

I want you to describe the wolverine bouncing along the creek bottom

Bob Swerer Jr.

May 24, 1971. Clear, calm and 25 degrees. At last a clear calm morning. I was up at 4:45. The surface of the lake was like concrete. I fooled around shooting a few feet of film and didn't get traveling until seven. I experimented at making some titles for this year's film, "The Frozen North," and frozen it really is. RLP

One day in the late fall my father and I were out looking for moose to film. We were six or seven miles from Dick Proenneke's cabin in an area where he said we might have some luck. After searching around a bit we found a nice big bull that had three or four cows with him. It was the rutting season and the bull was closely tending the cows. We moved in as close as we could with our big equipment and began filming the moose. But we pushed our luck a little too far and made the mistake of getting between the bull and the cows. Suddenly the bull moose became really agitated and charged us. In the process of trying to get away I got tangled up in the thick brush and went down on my knees. I was just waiting for this big bull to run over the top of my back. In the end, we got behind some trees and escaped, but the bull knocked over our camera and tripod in his rage.

The next day we saw Dick and he wanted to know if we'd found any moose. We sat in front of his cabin and I told him what had happened. Dick seemed to take note of the fact that I wasn't wearing my cap because he always had some kind of hat on. I explained that the charge had happened so fast that when I was scrambling in the brush I lost my ball cap. He wanted to know where that incident took place and all the details. We showed him the footage that we had gotten of this big bull before he had charged. Dick was amused; he really got a kick out of the whole event.

We left Twin Lakes a few days later. After I had been home for three or four weeks I got this little box in the mail. It was not an ordinary box. It was all molded out of cardboard and I could tell it was carefully handmade. I opened it up and there was my ball cap along with a letter from Dick. In this letter he described how he had hiked down the lake six or seven miles to the place I had described where the bull moose had charged us. He went on to say that he searched back and forth, back and forth, for most of the morning looking for my ball cap. And finally he found it. Then he put the cap on his head and he hiked back to his cabin. He made the box and sent the cap back to me because he thought that I would like to have it returned, although at that time I didn't really think anything about its loss.

What a thoughtful gesture it was for him to do that. Dick spent the whole morning searching for an old ball cap that wasn't that important to me but which he thought might be. To this day I still have that ball cap and his letter describing how he searched high and low for it, how thick the brush was, and how excited he was when he finally found it.

* * *

I grew up and spent most of my time out in the Colorado Mountains. The first time I heard about Dick Proenneke was when I was sixteen or seventeen years old and in high school. One day I came across a book by Sam Keith about a man living alone in the wilderness of Alaska and filming wildlife. That struck a chord with me, so I bought the book and after reading it I decided that his life was something I'd like to emulate.

My Dad and I were making films when I was just a kid. That was our love, just like it was for Dick. I think that's why we admired Dick long before we met him. The three of us had a lot in common, shooting film and watching wildlife. We liked to hike the hills and valleys with our 8-millimeter movie cameras. After we collected enough footage we would edit it and put together our films. We did this much for our own enjoyment. It was a hobby that eventually turned into a profession.

Many years later we eventually made a trip to Alaska to make a film. Believe it or not, after doing a lot of research we choose Twin Lakes as our destination. Because so much time had gone by we'd either forgotten or didn't realize that Dick Proenneke lived in that part of

Alaska. It wasn't until we actually got into the Twin Lakes area that we heard about a man that lived in this remote area. We set up our camp near a stream between the two lakes and really didn't give it any more thought until one evening when we were standing on the shoreline and a canoe approached. Of all the people to show up, it was Dick Proenneke! He stepped out of his canoe and introduced himself and then it all came together. I realized that this was the very man that I had read about when I was sixteen years old. It was now twenty-five years later, and just by chance he pulled up in his canoe in front of our camp.

That night was the first of many long visits with Dick. We were there with some pretty sophisticated video camera equipment and Dick was just enthralled. He was used to using old wind up 8- and 16-millimeter cameras, so when he saw our equipment, he couldn't ask us enough questions about it. He was so curious about video. Because he'd only worked with film he didn't know anything about it.

For the next couple of weeks we hiked together. He wanted to show us some of his favorite spots. He loved to look through our camera, and whenever we filmed something we could instantly rewind the tape and he could actually see what we were getting. Because he was so excited about our equipment we actually let him use our camera to photograph some Dall sheep.

He took us to all the usual places that he shared with guests. The hike up to Teetering Rock turned out to be interesting. He had a long pole that he made strictly to take up to the Teetering Rock. It was about eight feet long and it had a 16-penny nail taped to the end of it. He would lay that pole across the rock in such a way that when it moved the 16-penny nail would dip down and touch another rock. That allowed you to count exactly how many times the rock teetered. I swear we spent two hours up there and we would do it over and over. Whenever two of us would come up with a different count he'd say, "Hmm, let's do it again."

As we were sitting there playing with Teetering Rock I turned around and over my left shoulder was this huge bull moose. It was standing on a slope not more than seventy-five yards away. This was during the rut, so he was pretty bold and he was watching us. I turned and to Dick and said, "We've got company."

Dick turned around and couldn't believe his eyes. After all the years he'd spent trudging around these lakes trying to film large bull moose, one snuck up behind him while he is playing with his favorite rock. He got as big a kick out of that as we did.

When we got down to the cabin I told Dick, "You know, we have to get some video footage of that bull". Dick's eyes lit up at that suggestion. He said, "I'm going to get him down in the water." My Dad and I were skeptical, but Dick sounded serious. He crafted a plan and told us what to do. He said, "If you want to get some really good footage of a bull moose swimming in the lake, you guys take your raft and follow the shoreline up from my cabin about three or four hundred yards." And then he said, "I'm going to go up on the Hump and herd that moose down to you."

We followed Dick's instructions and got our camera gear all set up and paddled up the lake, which was smooth as glass. It was a beautiful day. We could see everything that was going on because we were a hundred yards off shore. We watched as Dick, walking stick in hand, hiked up and approached the bull moose. Dick was on a mission, and at first he looked like the more aggressive of the two. He was determined to herd that bull moose down to the edge of the lake and get him into the water so we could film it swimming in the lake.

As Dick closed in we could tell the bull didn't like the plan, and he wasn't any happier than the moose that had chased us a few days earlier. He was in rut, wearing a crown of impressive antlers, and wasn't in the mood for being herded, especially by a skinny man holding an equally skinny stick. The bull took charge of the situation and actually ended up herding Dick. It was entertaining to watch. Dick up there swinging his walking stick trying to scare a bull moose that wouldn't scare. In the end, it was Dick that came walking down to the lake. And when we last saw it, the moose had gone back to whatever it was doing before this whole episode started. Experiences like that I remember as if they were yesterday.

* * *

After we had met Dick at Twin Lakes we corresponded often by mail and when possible, telephone. That was very enjoyable as well and I learned so much just having conversations with him on the phone. I really loved talking to him. I was very curious, and I would ask him a lot of questions about animals and this and that. We also would go out and visit him. We made a few trips after he had moved to Hemet, California with his brother Raymond.

Over the years we continued to talk about film and equipment. That's when he told us about all this old film he had shot of building his cabin and the wildlife in the Twin Lakes area. He said, "You know, if you guys would be interested in putting together some of my film, I would like other people to see it." Dick was very proud of his films and he thought he had the greatest wildlife footage that ever was. He wanted us to do something with the film because he knew we had the expertise in film editing and production. All the film he had shot was silent, so both he and I knew we would have the task of adding sound.

In addition to the challenge of editing and adding sound to the film, we faced the challenge of communicating with Dick through the mail and periodic phone calls. When we had questions about a segment of film and what he would prefer to see, and in what sequence, we had to talk to him about it. So between him and Raymond we spent a lot of time talking about his films.

A little known and underappreciated fact is that Raymond was really the photographer in the Proenneke family. From the very beginning, even before Dick went up to Twin Lakes, Raymond was the one that had the knowledge of photography. It was his hobby and passion. He passed his knowledge and enthusiasm for photography on to Dick because he thought Dick should be recording the exciting adventures he was experiencing. It just wouldn't have happened without Raymond. He taught Dick how to use a movie camera, purchased all the equipment, and did much of the film processing and cataloging back in California. Ray was really the wind beneath Dick's wings. We can all be thankful for that.

While Raymond may have taught Dick the basics of photography, after Dick was at Twin Lakes he had to learn the rest by trial and error. His first attempts at filming were pretty crude. In those days cameras were entirely manual. All the exposure settings had to be manually dialed in and sometimes Dick would set his aperture at the wrong setting or he might have a problem with the camera, such as light leaking into the back. He had no capability to review the film there at Twin Lakes so months and months would go by during which he would shoot film that was drastically over-exposed or out of focus. Then he would send it to Raymond, who would look at it and write back, "Dick, you better try this." A lot of film went to waste because it was just not watchable. We have thousands and thousands of feet of such footage. Great exciting subject matter that you read about in his journals but sadly, it's unusable.

The initial film we put together was *Alaska Silence and Solitude.* That material was taken from our first filming trip to Twin Lakes and our first meeting with Dick Proenneke. Our intent with that film was to portray the scenery, our adventure with the local wildlife, and our meeting with Dick. When we showed him the film he really liked it.

The Frozen North was the next film, and one that we put together at Dick's request. He wanted us to do something with his film footage, so he wrote Raymond and asked him to send the original footage to us in Colorado. Raymond had already given it the title *The Frozen North* and had roughly edited and assembled a big reel of film.

After we took a look at what Raymond had sent I was firmly convinced that I wanted to have Dick do the narration. So I wrote to Dick and told him about my plans for the film. This kicked off a long process because I'd have to write him a letter and in turn wait for him to respond. Given the mail connection between Colorado and a remote cabin in bush Alaska, an answer could take a month or more. Whenever he would get to Port Alsworth or return to California to see Raymond we would talk by phone. Whenever that rare opportunity arose we did a lot of talking.

I thought it was important that Dick narrate the film, because who better to describe the scenes than Dick himself? But how would I do this when Dick was 3,000 miles from my sound studio in Colorado? My solution was to mail a little portable Sony tape recorder to Dick. It was a good quality tape recorder that had a microphone with a stand on it. After studying the film for some time, I would describe certain scenes to Dick. It had been years since he last saw some of the film and there was a lot of footage that I don't think he had ever seen before.

In my letters I would tell Dick how we put a scene together and describe it. Then I would tell him how long he needed to talk. For example, I might say, "Dick, the scene is thirty seconds long and I want you to describe the wolverine bouncing along the creek bottom as best as you can from memory." I would also invite him to add anything else that he could think of that was pertinent to that scene. So over and over I wrote descriptions of all the scenes in the film.

When Dick received my instructions and the tape recorder he would sit in his cabin and start describing the scenes on tape. Most people who have watched *The Frozen North* find it rather comical because it's apparent that Dick is reading from text. But like everything else he did, Dick took this assignment very seriously and he would do it over and over. When he reached the point of frustration he'd write me a letter and say, "I hate my voice. I can't do this. This is for a professional." I kept pushing him. I would write him back and say, "Dick, it's important that we have your voice with his film. You're Dick Proenneke."

Never one to give up, Dick even decided to pack up his tape recorder and take it outside to try some "live" recordings. We didn't know what to expect when we played that tape but we listened intently. On the tape we could hear him crunching along on the ice. He was talking at the same time that he was watching a big dark brown bear that he initially thought was a black bear. As Dick watched the bear he narrated a play-by-play account of the bear's movements and actions. Then, all of a sudden, we heard the ice crunch and Dick went through the lake ice, tape recorder still running. I guess he went in up to his waist but he saved the tape recorder.

If that weren't amusing enough, in the middle of narrating outdoor scenes Dick would ask, "Bob, how does this sound? I'm six inches away from the microphone. Does this sound any better to you?" Every time I listen to those original tapes it's altogether comical, nostalgic, and heartwarming to hear him talking and re-reading his accounts. "Oh, that doesn't sound too good. Let me try that again." And then he'd say, "Let me step outside the cabin. I'm going to move, the wind's blowing so I've got to get out of the wind."

The process of adding sound to that film went on for many months. The next time you watch *The Frozen North* think of Dick and how he's narrating it. In the end, we took the best of what he said and plugged it into the film. It wouldn't be what it is without Dick's voice.

After we finished the film I sent a copy to Dick. He wrote back to thank us and say how anxious he was to watch it. Easier said than done; he had to wait for a ride back to Port Alsworth. The days must have passed slowly for him, having the film and not being able to watch it. Eventually the Park Service picked him up and he was able to view it. In letters he wrote to me afterward I recall that that he thought it was a real good film. But he also mentioned that the Park Service was critical because we didn't mention the name of the Park or the specific location. The reason we chose not to do so was that we thought we were doing Dick a favor by not revealing the location of his cabin. We assumed that Dick didn't want that information out there because it would bring too many people to the area.

Dick was quite a guy, and we miss him so much. It's amazing how many people that man has inspired. We hear it constantly from people over the Internet or the telephone. After talking about the films we've put together from Dick's footage most go on to tell us about how Dick has touched their lives. We've had people call from the hospital and say, "My husband is dying of cancer and all he wants to do is watch Dick Proenneke in his hospital bed. That's what's keeping him alive."

We hear things like that all the time, and it's very touching. It just gives you goose bumps. To many his journals are almost like their Bible. I received a letter here at the office not long ago that I saved. It's from a soldier over in Afghanistan and it's about ten or twelve pages long. In it he writes how Dick Proenneke changed him as a man and how thoughts of Dick keep him going during difficult times. Many are simply inspired by the way Dick lived, his self-sufficient lifestyle, and every-day pleasures that made him so happy. We have a lot of people tell us they have to watch the film at least once a week just to keep going. And they never get tired of it, that's the impact that Dick Proenneke can have on people.

In 1991 film makers and producers Bob Swerer, Jr. and his father first met Dick Proenneke while they were in the Twin Lakes region to explore the area and film wildlife. Their mutual affection for photographing nature and the wilderness forged a close and long friendship. In 1997, the Swerers returned to Alaska to visit with Proenneke. With more than 3,000 feet of film shot by Dick, and his meticulous and poetic journals entries detailing his adventures at Twin Lakes, the Swerers produced four one-hour films.

The fish knew that we were having a party today

Alison Woodings

I worked one summer for Mark and Sandy Lang at their Lake Clark Inn at Port Alsworth. Dick would come down to do road grading for Glen or Bee Alsworth on one of the runways. I first met him because he stayed at the lodge when he was in Port Alsworth. Then the next summer I worked for Chuck and Sara Hornberger at their Koksetna Lodge on Lake Clark, and Dick came over for a visit. He invited me to visit him when I was finished at the Hornbergers. I think of Dick as a kindred spirit. I grew up here in Alaska. My backyard was a mountain, my front yard was a river, and my best friend were the trails. Dick loved those things as much as anybody I'd ever met.

At Mark and Sandy's lodge we always had fishing guests so there would usually be a large group of people with a lot talking, and Dick would tell stories. I don't remember any of his stories but people were interesting to him.

One night, when I was staying at Mark and Sandy's lodge, I went up to a friend's house because her husband was gone and there had been a bear lurking around the house. That's a story in itself. The bear did show up and we whispered to each other, "I hear the bear." We put a flashlight to the window and were confronted by an enormous bear head. He was getting into the cooler on the deck and we were shining the light right in his face. So my friend got the gun and I went around the other side of the house to scare him away. When she popped out the little door to shoot at the bear he ran away. But I had to walk home.

I called a co-worker at Mark and Sandy's to escort me home and he said, "No way. I'm not going up there. There are bears out there." And so I walked home by myself. Dick gave that co-worker hell for that. Chivalry was very much a part of Dick's nature.

One of the pilots for Mark and Sandy told me this story about Dick: There were some kids trying to build a fire on the beach in the wind, and they weren't having much luck. Dick was watching but not saying anything. Then he casually walked by and said in the most nonchalant way, "If one were to build a fire in the wind one might put some rocks in front for protection from the wind." And then he walked off. He wasn't telling them what to do or telling them they were stupid, but he was just informing them.

That second fall I came to visit Dick over my birthday. It's always a beautiful time of year and those days at Twin Lakes were was almost dreamlike, just a really sweet time.

I got to stay in Spike's cabin and we just spent time together. We went hiking and canoeing. I still paddle the way Dick showed me. There's the typical "J" stroke, which I knew, but Dick had a particular way that he twisted the paddle. So that's something I've kept with me.

Canoeing with Dick was easy. We paddled at a steady but slow pace. And conversation, when it came out or not, was very comfortable. Dick seemed content either talking or not talking. He always spoke well of people and talked about the Park Service. He told some of his stories, like trying to take pictures of owls and he mentioned his winter walks.

When we were canoeing, I asked him, "Do you get lonely or is this enough?"

He said, "I never get lonely."

But then he wrote me a letter afterward and said, "After you left I felt lonely."

Dick made my birthday a very special day. I woke up and walked down to his cabin.

"Well, happy birthday," he said. "What would you like to do on your birthday?"

"I want to make a knife with you," I said.

He thought about it for a bit then he said, "Just a minute."

He left and went to his shed and when he came back in he gave me a knife. He said, "I don't have all the materials to make a good knife right now and it takes too long. You're not going to be here that long. I think we should go on a hike today."

So we got ready to go on a long hike but before we left we did my favorite kind of fishing. He took some line and threw it in the lake with a hook and we took off hiking. I hate fishing because to me it's boring. I like to do something more active.

We hiked up behind his cabin. Way back up. I think he said it was nine miles. He always let me walk first, which was really nice. I like walking first and it honored me that someone who walked hundreds of miles every year let me take the lead.

A lot of people know that he made sourdough pancakes for breakfast, but his lunches too were always sourdough pancakes with some peanut butter. He just made extra, and that was what we ate on our hike that day.

Once we got to the upper end of the valley Dick said, "See that glacier over there?"

 "Yeah," I replied.

He said, "That glacier doesn't have a name. I'm going to name it Alison Glacier."

I don't know if it's official or not, but years later I learned that the National Park Service stuck that name on their map.

When we got back to Dick's cabin there was a very large lake trout on the line and Dick made much of it. He said, "Oh, the fish knew that we were having a party today." So we had trout for dinner. It was just a wonderful day.

The day after my birthday we went to the other side of the lake and picked blueberries. Those blueberries were the best ever. I'd love to go back just to pick blueberries.

Dick told me that I was the first person he'd ever seen pick blueberries lying down! But they were so plentiful you could just lie there and chat and enjoy the sun while you filled your bucket. I don't think Dick ever thought of that before. I don't think he was the lying down kind of guy. He was always busy doing something.

I felt very honored and respected by him. It was a good feeling to spend time with him, someone that loved just being outside. I know he was proud, really proud, of what he'd accomplished but he didn't brag about it.

Alison never returned to Twin Lakes but she corresponded with Dick as she worked her way through college and traveled around the United States and Europe. Before settling in the Matanuska Susitna Valley where she grew up, she taught school in Tanana, Ketchikan, and Fairbanks.

What do you think I piled all that snow up there for

Lee Fink

October 7, 1977. Snowing, blowing up and 27 degrees. Plane day coming up so this would be a good day to write letters. Since June 10 I have used nearly two and half bottles of ink. Paper nearly 500, 8 x 11 1/2 sheets in the last two seasons at Twin Lakes. I wrote till noon, then took a break. RLP

"Wow, there's hardly any snow up here," said Leon Alsworth as we descended toward Twin Lakes in the National Park Service's Super Cub. It was the day before Thanksgiving and we were taking Dick his mail. We had the plane stuffed with five large bags of mail and boxes. Some of it included early Christmas presents. The ice was not thick enough to land on the lake by his cabin so we talked with Dick on the radio, hemming and hawing about what to do. Finally, we all agreed on a plan to drop it. But Dick said, "Wait until I pile up some snow."

We circled the Hope Creek delta near his cabin and watched as Dick mounded up a big pile of snow in a flat open area. After a few minutes he stopped, pulled out his radio and said, "Okay, see if you can hit that." Leon lined up the plane into the wind for our approach. It was a cold, windy day and I remember Leon saying, "Well, I'm going to have to correct for the wind."

The mail bags were behind my seat in the baggage compartment, and the only way I could retrieve them was to unbuckle my seat belt, reach around and pull them up over my shoulder. When I dropped it, the first bag went off course and bounced across the gravel that Dick had exposed in making his snow pile.

As we turned around for our second drop Dick's voice came over the radio. "Well, by golly, if you can't do any better than that, what do you think I piled all that snow up there for? You guys were supposed to throw them on the snow pile!"

We got better after that. I think the next four mail drops hit the snow pile dead on. And he was pretty happy with that.

When we next saw Dick two months later he was sporting a new pedometer that his brother had sent him. He said, "Oh, look at this here, my brother Raymond sent me this for Christmas." I looked at it and couldn't believe my eyes. That pedometer had 540 miles on it. That was in two months! He walked 540 miles in two months. I'd never thought about it, but it just didn't seem possible that in the middle of winter a man could walk that many miles.

Another memorable mail delivery occurred late in the fall during one of Dick's final years at Twin Lakes. The wind was gusting and the Upper Lake was too rough for a floatplane landing. We found a sheltered spot on the Lower Lake and landed there. Before touching down we called Dick on the radio to say that we were going to cache his mail there for him to retrieve after the lake settled down. I can't remember why but Dick was adamant on getting his mail that day. He launched his canoe and paddled down lake to meet us. We parked at the upper end of Lower Lake and carried his mail and packages a third of a mile to the lower end of the Upper Lake.

While we waited there for Dick it kept getting winder and windier. Finally we saw him coming toward us riding up and down over the crests of large rolling whitecaps. I said to Leon, "This doesn't look good."

When he reached shore we pulled the canoe up on the beach but not before the prop on his "gas paddle," a 4-horsepower outboard, struck a rock and sheared a pin. Now we had another problem to solve. We had to jury rig a new shear pin for the motor or he was going to have to walk home, something he didn't seem to want to do that day.

Leon and I were thinking that walking back was the better of the two possibilities but Dick was pretty intent on returning home the same way he left home. In his canoe, and with his mail. Somehow we put the prop back together with a homemade shear pin. By the time we pushed him off shore there were two foot swells coming down the Upper Lake. Leon and I didn't say anything to each other as we watched him slowly chugging up lake with that old outboard. I can remember thinking, "Oh, man. If he ever capsizes or drowns out there in that lake, I hope it's not today."

* * *

I first met Dick Proenneke in the summer of 1984 when I was based in Port Alsworth with the Bureau of Land Management (BLM) field survey crew. One of our local assignments was to survey and mark a five-acre parcel of land on Upper Twin Lake as a native allotment selection for Mary Alsworth. When we landed our helicopter at the mouth of Hope Creek Dick Proenneke met us. He was friendly but somewhat concerned that we were going to cut a survey line around his cabin and the surrounding area when he hadn't even put in the claim.

Eventually he agreed to assist us in cutting trees and brush around the perimeter of the 5-acre parcel. Although the survey was completed, the parcel was never conveyed to Mary Alsworth.

When the field season ended that summer I left BLM but remained in Port Alsworth where I worked on acquiring my private and commercial airplane pilot licenses. Many of my early flights involved taking Dick back and forth between Twin Lakes and Port Alsworth. Dick's talents were in high demand by local residents at Lake Clark. He had an exceptional mind for machinery and the ability to solve almost any construction or building problem.

In the 1980s there was very little or no radio communication with Dick at Twin Lakes. I would usually show up at his cabin unannounced any time of day with a request for his assistance. If the American flag was flying on the pole above his cabin it usually meant Dick was home. If the flag was not out you could always go in the cabin and find a map on his desk that had a pin placed on the destination that he was traveling to on that day.

Dick was frequently asked to repair the road grader that was used to maintain the Port Alsworth runway or some other piece of machinery that nobody locally had the time or talent to try to nurse back to life. What amazed me was that he came out of the wilderness of Twin Lakes where he'd been doing absolutely nothing mechanical for weeks or months on end and then would just dive right into tearing down a diesel engine or replacing the brake pads on a dump truck.

Whatever the problem, when I described it to Dick he would usually look up quizzically and say, "Hmm. Hmm. Well I suppose we can do that." Before we left he would saunter around the cabin and throw a few things in his army duffel bag. Finally, he would "secure" the cabin by putting the bear shutters on the windows and storing food in his cool box or cache.

As far as I knew few people ever paid Dick for his talents but they would usually send him home with plenty of fresh supplies. He was always anxious to return home after the project was completed.

I always enjoyed visiting Dick in winter. If Dick was home he was usually standing out on the ice as I made my final approach to land. One spring I landed after Dick had assured me over the radio that the ice was over eighteen inches thick. I was flying the Cessna 185 on wheels and after I landed I parked a couple hundred feet offshore from his beach just in case the ice was weak along the shore. I think I'd thrown the engine cover on because it was fairly cold. We visited for a while and then started walking back out to the airplane. When we got close, the left wheel suddenly dropped through the ice. Just as suddenly the left side of the airplane settled so that the top of the tire was level with the top of the ice.

I was speechless, and Dick said, "Oh, what's going to happen here?" We just stood there looking at the plane. Was the other wheel going to fall through? Was the whole airplane going to go down?

After we regained our senses we circled the plane and looked at the ice. It seemed pretty solid but there must have been a weak spot under the plane because a square-shaped piece of ice popped up where the tire fell though. Dick trotted back to his woodshed and gathered some boards and a couple of stout spruce poles. We used the poles to leverage the left side of the plane up and slipped the boards under the tire. With the tire up it was no problem taxiing out of what could have been an extended stay with Dick.

After freeze-up visitation dropped off at Twin Lakes and I don't know that he was any happier to see people then, but in winter he could go for weeks or even months without a visit. On cold winter days we would sit by the warm wood stove and he'd have a million things to tell me. He had a knack for picking up on a conversation at exactly the same place where he had left off weeks earlier. More often than not, I had little or no recollection of what we had talked about, much less where we had left off! Of course I never said that to him. I tried to play along until I finally caught up and remembered.

He always had his "girls" sitting there on the wood stove, the two perfectly rounded rocks that he used as bed warmers. If you sat there long enough and kept glancing at them he would eventually look at you and say, "Yeah, go ahead. You can grab one of the girls." I'd put it in my lap and enjoy the sensation that a warm stone can provide on a cold day. In winter he was content if the air temperature in his cabin was above freezing three feet above the floor. That was his goal, keep it above freezing three feet off the floor.

Dick enjoyed the simple life that he lived. He seemed to have achieved all his worldly needs early in his years at Twin Lakes and thereafter he never really changed. He didn't keep adding and adding personal belongings like most people do in life. He never acquired battery-operated tools to replace his hand tools or a gasoline-powered pump to replace his water bucket. He just kept it simple. Perhaps that's one of the most unique traits he had.

Dick always seemed to enjoy having visitors and even overnight guests, provided they didn't overstay their welcome. Female visitors who took it upon themselves to give Dick advice on cooking, housekeeping, or his diet were not always popular. I recall Dick's words after one such extended visit. "What do these women think I do when they are not here? I'm perfectly capable of taking care of myself. I live here three hundred sixty five days a year and get along just fine with nobody telling me what I need to do." I always thought that was pretty funny. I guess it was probably a good thing he never got married.

* * *

It was always amusing when Dick left his Twin Lakes wilderness behind and traveled to the big city of Anchorage. During his final years prostrate problems forced him to make an emergency trip to the

Alaska Regional Hospital. After someone flew him from Twin Lakes to Port Alsworth I traveled with him on Lake Clark Air to Anchorage. Later that evening I checked him into the emergency room of the hospital. The first stop was registration, where I had the challenging task of filling out a small mountain of paperwork. As I worked away asking Dick question after question, his attention seemed more focused on all the medical equipment and gadgets that surrounded us. "Dick," I said, "we've got to do all this. How much money do you have?" He replied, "Oh, I think I have about $1,800.00 in my checking account."

Dick didn't have any health insurance and only a modest income from his annual Alaska Permanent Fund Dividend and his monthly Alaska Longevity Bonus payment. Filling in his whole financial section left a lot of blank space. There were a lot of questions for which neither of us had an answer. But we slowly made progress. I turned over the last page and asked Dick one more question. "Do you have any stocks or bonds?"

"Well, you know, let's see. I've got some stocks," Dick replied.

Surprised and at the same time relieved, I asked, "Oh, really, they want to know what they're worth."

Dick paused for and moment, then replied "Oh, man. My brother Raymond bought those for me in the1940s, I think he bought them from General Motors. "

I said, "Do you have any idea what they are worth?"

"Oh, I don't know. The last time I asked Raymond he said they were maybe worth a couple hundred thousand."

My mind suddenly went as blank as the form in front of me. I thought, you've been eating beans and oatmeal for the last thirty years and you have a couple hundred thousand dollars in stocks?

After Dick was discharged from the hospital he stayed with my wife, Shannon, and me for a few days before heading back to Twin Lakes. He was riding around Anchorage with me one day while I was running errands. I needed some cash so I stopped at an ATM next to a Safeway grocery store. I said, "Dick, I need to get a little cash."

"Hmm. How you going to do that?" asked Dick.

I said, "Well, I'll get it out of this ATM machine here. I'll just put my card in there and get some cash." Dick got out of the car and followed along, eyeing me like a lynx watching a snowshoe hare. I inserted my card, entered my pin number, and pulled out some cash.

Dick was totally astonished. He began a methodical inspection of the machine, similar to what he might have done had it been a new Caterpillar dozer. He examined the back, front, and sides of the ATM. Finally he asked, "Well, now. How does that work?"

Meanwhile another customer approached and I began to worry that someone was going to get suspicious, thinking Dick was trying to break into it. I said, "Well, you put your card in there and it accesses your bank account and gives you money."

"Wow! What keeps some big guy from coming up and whacking you on the head and taking your card?"

I said, "You've got to have a PIN number."

"Oh, what's a PIN number?"

I said, "That's a personal code you put in after you put your card in. You know, it's a number that confirms your identity."

Dick said, "Well. I'll be."

So ended Dick's first trip to Anchorage in thirteen years.

After building up his flight hours as Dick's chauffeur, Lee Fink moved on to become a natural resource specialist-pilot for Lake Clark National Park and Preserve. He later became a district ranger-pilot and eventually chief ranger, a position he held until his retirement in 2015. But over the years he rarely missed the opportunity to be chauffer, including the day he flew former President Jimmy Carter and First Lady Rosalyn to sample grayling in the Tazimina River. Of course it was to commemorate the 20th anniversary of the Alaska National Interest Lands Conservation Act (ANILCA).

Seven, One, Eight . . . Upper Lake

Alan Bennett

"Boy the wind is blowing here this morning, down lake and gusting, temperature at the cabin is coming up, eighteen degrees now and starting to snow; what's it doing down there?"

Dick Proenneke's morning radio call marked the beginning of another day at the National Park Service's field headquarters in Port Alsworth. Dick had a distinctive voice. His speech was gentle with a rhythmic melody. It lingered in your mind, like the call of a loon or the howl of a wolf.

In the early 1980s Dick was made an official backcountry National Park Service volunteer and soon thereafter he was issued a hand-held Park Service radio. This was a major change, because for the first time he was connected to the outside world. I'm not sure what Dick enjoyed more, the ability to chat with his friends in Port Alsworth about the weather, wolves, and bears, or the challenge of making the radio work.

Given the National Parks' VHF repeater-based radio system that was in place during the 1980s and early 1990s, it was a miracle that it worked at all. For Dick to transmit and receive from his cabin, the radio signal had to reach a repeater twenty-four miles to the south-east on the west end of Lake Clark Pass. That repeater relayed the signal to the Park Service base station in Port Alsworth.

The list of obstacles standing in the way of Dick's ability to call out on his radio was long and changed hourly. Wind, rain, snow, fog, air temperature, repeater malfunction, repeater icing, radio malfunction, weak battery . . . all contributed to making Dick's contact with the outside world a challenge. Situated at the mouth of Hope Creek and surrounded by mountains, Dick's cabin was on the edge of what radio technicians would call, "a transmission dead spot."

Over the years, Dick tinkered with all sorts of external antennae in an effort to improve reception. But more often than not, the only sure-

fire way to reach Park headquarters on the radio was to gain elevation. Fortunately, gaining elevation was something Dick was very
good at. Climbing 500 feet to the top of the Hump behind his cabin
usually helped. But when all else failed, he had to hike two and half
miles down lake and climb up to the bench at the entrance to Low
Pass. From there he could hit the Park's other repeater, which is forty-
two miles to the northwest in the Bonanza Hills. Even then, if everything magically worked, Park Service staff had to be in the office in
Port Alsworth, and they had to remember to turn on the radio in the
morning.

During my first year with the Park Service, office staff were few in
number. There were four of us squeezed into a small house that the
NPS had purchased from Babe Alsworth's oldest son, Wayne (Bee).
Two downstairs rooms served as offices. Pilot-ranger Leon Alsworth
and I shared a former bedroom and Chief Ranger Joe Fowler used
what once was the kitchen. An upstairs living space served as the
"operations center," supporting functions that were spread over half
a dozen buildings in most Parks. District Ranger Clair Roberts occupied a small office space behind this room and was first in line to
answer the radio when Dick faithfully called in with his morning report.

Radio protocol was informal in those years. Dick's call sign of "Upper
Lake" was fine with us, and became etched in the minds of those who
answered his calls. As one might expect, Dick's radio calls were
timely and organized. First he reported weather conditions; second,
wildlife sightings and movements, with special attention to wolves,
bears, sheep, and caribou; and third, an accounting of aircraft and
visitors to Twin Lakes. Dick usually had as many questions as he did
answers. He was always curious about the Lake Clark weather, what
was going on at Port Alsworth, and the mail, always the mail.

Dick's voice had a way of grabbing one's attention. Busy as he could
be, I can recall Joe Fowler ending a telephone conversation early because he wanted to listen to Dick's Twin Lakes report. I often stopped
what I was doing and positioned myself halfway up the stairs. From
there I could more clearly hear the conversation and at the same time
I was concealed so that no one could see that I was listening to Dick
and not working. Over the years Dick used his radio in ways that

proved invaluable to the NPS. He reported poaching cases, helped visitors contact Park headquarters, radioed weather conditions to Park pilots, and aided distressed hikers and pilots.

Making radio contact with Park headquarters by radio was at its worst in the dead of winter. Dick's solar powered battery chargers were useless, and ice storms frequently coated the repeaters. Days, and on occasions weeks, would go by without hearing from him. Then one morning Joe would walk into the office, look at Leon and me and say, "Maybe you two should go up and check on Dick." Those words no sooner left his mouth than we were out the door.

* * *

Before I arrived at Lake Clark my familiarity with Dick was limited to a reading of *One Man's Wilderness*. My excitement and enthusiasm for meeting him grew daily with each of his morning radio calls. Weeks passed, and finally that opportunity arrived. It was the last week of November in 1991 when Leon and I were doing a moose count north of Twin Lakes. We would stop in at Dick's on the way home. It was a calm and clear day, and after hours of flying over the snow-covered valleys and plateaus near the headwaters of the Mulchatna River it was easy to imagine that you were alone in the world.

As we headed south, the Chilikadrotna River came into view and Leon eased the Super Cub to the left and up the north side of Lower Twin Lake. As we approached the connecting stream between the lower and upper lake Dick's voice rang out on the radio, "Leon, is that you?"

"Yeah, hi Dick, we're coming in, how is the ice?" Leon replied. We were flying 200 feet above the trees and five miles from his cabin. I wondered how he knew it was the park plane.

"Oh, the ice is good, eight inches, some small drifts. Stay on my trail," Dick replied.

"Okay, see you in a bit, I've got Alan along," said Leon.

As we began a low approach Leon glanced up at the Cub's thermometer, "Wow, its cold here, minus twenty-one," he said. That was twenty degrees colder than where we were just a few minutes ago. Looking ahead, I saw something unexpected. A runway! Dick had the four corners of a 200-foot long strip marked out on the ice with wooden crosses. He had also made multiple passes up and down the center on snowshoes to flatten any large snowdrifts.

It was a smooth landing, and when I crawled out of the Cub and greeted Dick he said, "You must be Alan; I've been waiting for you." Dick pointed me toward his cabin while Leon tied an insulated blanket over the engine cowling of the Super Cub. As we walked up a neatly shoveled path to the lakeshore and then up toward the cabin Dick remarked, "Snowpack is eighteen inches right now." Hastily he opened the door and I stomped the snow off my boots and stepped inside. I was greeted by a warm blast of humid air that immediately fogged up my eyeglasses. Nearsighted and temporarily blinded, I knew enough to freeze in position and not risk stumbling over something on the floor.

When I finally managed to clear my glasses, I looked up to see Dick at his desk busily stuffing letters into envelopes, then licking and sealing them one at a time. Leon had slipped in and was sitting on Dick's lower bunk. The two of them had a rapid-fire conversation going about moose, wolves, and who was doing what with airplanes in Port Alsworth. I was content to listen and look. The close bond between Dick and Leon was evident, not unlike uncle and nephew or even father and son. The whole experience of standing in Dick's cabin for the first time brought on a sensory overload that temporarily left me speechless.

After fifteen minutes or so I looked around for a place to sit. Dick didn't offer me anything, and the bunk that Leon was sitting on was piled high with clothes and boxes. Out of the corner of my eye I saw a small three-legged stool between the wood stove and his bunk. I stepped over in that direction and sat down. Perfect. I was right next to the warm stove and directly facing Dick. I didn't realize it at the time but that would be my perch from then on, every time I visited with Dick in his cabin.

After sealing his last envelope, Dick reached into a box under his desk and pulled out a skull. He turned to me and said, "Now Alan, you're a wildlife biologist, can you tell whether this is a male or a female wolverine?" He handed me the skull and I carefully looked it over, knowing full well that I was caught off guard and didn't have an answer. I might have had that answer a couple of decades earlier after I'd aced a graduate-level comparative vertebrate anatomy course. I pointed to the elevated ridge on the top of the skull and said, "I think the sagittal crest is longer on a male, so this might be a female, but I'm not sure." "Hmm," said Dick, which I interpreted to mean he was not impressed.

There were other skulls in the box that I instantly recognized, so in an effort to redeem myself I asked Dick, "I see you've got a few beaver skulls, a porcupine, and that's a real nice marten, where did you get that?" The conversation continued and ranged from moose calves to ptarmigan. I could have kept it going all night, but this would be a brief visit. In subzero temperatures, Leon had an uncanny ability to sense the cooling temperature of the oil in the engine of the Super Cub. When his internal alarm clock went off, he stood up, grabbed Dick's outgoing mail, and headed for the door.

Over the years those mail stops at Dick's fell into a routine. A visit in the cabin, a cup of tea, a hike, snowshoe, or canoe paddle up the lake if time and the weather permitted, and always the questions. Do parky (arctic ground) squirrels climb trees? Will cow caribou adopt calves that are not their own? I think Dick stored questions in his mind over the years and recycled them whenever a new biologist came to visit.

Dick usually had something he wanted us to check on once we were airborne and on our return flight to Port Alsworth. A moose kill down lake, signs of the wolf pack over by Emerson Creek, bands of nearby caribou, or backpackers. After we had checked things out we would report back to him by radio. Our aerial observation would either save him a hike or launch him off on a new one.

* * *

After Dick became a Park Service volunteer, the Port Alsworth post office combined Dick's mail with that of the park and personal mail of the park staff. Dick's reputation as prolific letter writer is widely known. Less well known was his reputation for accumulating incoming mail. As one of his mail handlers, I swear that for every letter Dick mailed he received two in return.

At headquarters the mail was sorted and pigeon-holed into a row of boxes that hung on the wall of a small hallway outside Clair's office. On any given day, Dick's mail could equal or exceed the sum of both Park and staff. In the weeks before Christmas, letters and parcel post boxes piled up like cordwood. Fans, friends and family would inundate Dick with gifts of candy, nuts, and all sorts of processed foods, most of which he wouldn't eat. One year in his journal he would write:

"My cabin and cache have been full to overflowing for quite some time and each new load makes me wonder where I will stow it all... I do appreciate everything but wish they would consider the poor miserable brush rat more fortunate than they and spend their money to beat death and taxes."RLP

It often seemed like Dick received the most mail at times when it was most challenging to deliver it. Depending upon the weather, there could be a prolonged period in late fall before Upper Twin Lake was frozen solid enough to support aircraft landings near Dick's cabin. Mail deliveries took many forms, depending on conditions: no ice, thin ice, or broken ice. Letters were placed in a nylon bag and dropped out of the window of the Park Super Cub as it passed over an unvegetated stretch of Hope Creek delta. Blaze orange surveyor flagging was tied to the bag in the event that the drop was off the mark and ended up in the spruce trees. Dick usually positioned himself in the drop zone, directed the pilot with his radio, and on a windless day with a perfectly timed drop, came close to catching the mail bag.

Boxes were another matter. When landings at his cabin were not possible, Dick placed his outgoing mail in a Blazo [fuel] can atop a beaver lodge on the southeast end of the Lower Lake near the mouth of Beech Creek. Because the lower lake was shallower, it froze weeks before the upper lake, allowing us to land and pick up his outgoing mail on the return trip. Occasionally, we would leave incoming boxes on the beaver lodge, but NOT without Dick's blessing. Subzero temperatures would freeze the contents even if Dick immediately took off on the eight-mile roundtrip to retrieve them.

I recall one particular delivery when Dick had been expecting a parcel from his brother Raymond. It contained adhesives and other contents that Dick did not want to freeze. When we reached Upper Twin Lake the temperature was minus ten degrees and dropping. As Leon circled Dick's cabin discussing the options with him over the radio, I fumbled though the mail bag and confirmed that yes, the small package from Raymond was in there. Landing on the Lower Lake and waiting for Dick to hike down was not an option because daylight was fading fast.

The ice in front of Dick's cabin was glassy smooth but barely a couple of inches thick. East of Carrithers's Point, sections of the lake remained open. Leon suggested that he could do a near shore touch-and-go and that I could gently toss the mailbag out the door of the cub. Dick seemed to like the idea. I wasn't so sure. Sitting in the back of a Super Cub wearing a helmet, bulky survival vest, and several layers of clothing makes it difficult enough to scratch your nose, let alone toss a mail bag out the door while sliding across the ice.

Leon said, "I'll tell you when to let it go," but warned: "Make sure you clear the skis." In my mind I wondered how Dick might react if his mail did a touch and go and flew back to Port Alsworth dangling from the right ski of a Super Cub. "Now," said Leon and I tossed the mail sack out the door. It bounced once, then slid across the ice like a hockey puck and came to rest a few feet from Dick's beach where it was eagerly grabbed by its recipient. Mail delivered!

* * *

"Onward and upward," said Dick as he stood and continued our climb up the side of a steep mountain. I never saw Dick wear a pack on day hikes. No water bottles, no trail mix, no extra clothing. If he ate anything during the hike it was usually a couple of left over sourdough hotcakes coated with peanut butter and honey. They were rolled up like a cigar and placed in his upper left shirt pocket. "Sticks of dynamite," he called them. Dick drank water from snowmelt streams using his cupped hand like a dipper. Higher up on the mountains he ate snow. If he removed a layer of clothing during a hike it was tied around his waist. He always carried a walking stick made from a sapling black spruce. It was both a walking aid and a push pole that he used to clear small rocks off caribou and sheep trails when crossing steep scree slopes.

Hiking behind Dick was both exhausting and relaxing. It was relaxing because I never had to worry about choosing the shortest or safest route, carrying a map, or finding my way back. During his first decade of hiking at Twin Lakes Dick carried a stop watch. He used it to measure hiking time-in-route to final destinations and landmarks along the way. Calculations were fine-tuned on successive hikes and compared to alternate routes used to reach the same destination. Over time his stopwatch, pedometer, and razor-sharp memory gave him the equivalent of an internal GPS. At any point during a hike Dick could answer the question: "How long before we reach the next canyon?"

Dick's hiking destinations often coincided with seasonal rhythms of the wildlife he closely watched. Caribou calving grounds, Dall sheep lambing and mineral licks, brown bear dens, red fox dens, hoary marmot dens, ptarmigan wintering grounds, and American Dipper nests were a few of the sites he lead me to. Dick marked special occasions such as his birthday, summer solstice, or New Year's Day with hikes to his favorite destinations.

Dick had an inquisitive mind and he was constantly searching for alternate routes to reach the same destination. He usually traveled different routes ascending and descending a mountain. Because winter snow and frozen creeks afforded travel that was not possible in summer, he often had both a winter and a summer route to most destinations. On my three hikes with Dick to the top of his beloved Falls Mountain he traveled a different route each time.

Winter never slowed Dick's hiking. He seemed to thrive on subzero temperatures. Wearing forty-two-inch long-tail snowshoes and weighing only 150 pounds, Dick floated on snow. I will never forget flying over Twin Lakes in winter and looking down at Dick's snowshoe tracks. Miles and miles of tracks radiated outward from his cabin like spokes on a wheel, crisscrossing both lakes and valleys. Most trails were straight as an arrow, looking more like they were made by a machine than by a man.

On one of our first winter hikes together I learned how he made all those straight trails. "There's a wolf-killed moose down lake, I want to go look at it," Dick said as I climbed out of the back seat of a Piper Super Cub.

"Sure," I replied—somewhat reluctantly given the minus ten-degree temperature. Before I could secure my snowshoes, Dick rocketed off like a wolverine after game, and with a steady lope to match. He seemed to take a visual fix on a distant landmark and marched straight for it. Miles and miles went by non-stop, and after an hour I began to realize that "down lake" actually meant "end of lake."

Finally we reached the kill site, where I found myself looking at a few scattered bones and a doormat-size chunk of hide. Obviously the wolves had revisited the carcass since Dick first found it. As I was thinking to myself, "We hiked all the way down here to see this,'" Dick looked across the lake and said "Well...since we're here let's go over to Emerson Creek and see if the Great Horned Owl is on its nest."

Once again I was following Dick as he marched straight across the lake toward the mouth of Emerson Creek and then straight up the frozen creek bed. Three miles later we entered a thick stand of timber, and when I finally caught up with Dick he was standing at the base of a tall cottonwood looking up at a large but empty stick nest. "I wonder if they moved farther up creek," said Dick, as I tried to think of an indirect way to tell him that it might be a good time to turn around without admitting that my feet were freezing. "I think it might be too early in the season for them to be incubating," I suggested, looking back in the direction of Dick's cabin.

"Hmm, maybe so," said Dick, and we turned around to backtrack down to the lakeshore. As we approached the shoreline and turned to head up lake we were greeted by a strong gusty wind. Blowing snow obscured all but the mountaintops as Dick set off on a bearing straight up the middle of the lake. After four nonstop miles with snow biting at our faces, we finally stepped inside a warm and welcome cabin. "Oh boy, that sure was a good hike," proclaimed Dick.

* * *

"Seven, one, eight...Upper Lake." Dick's voice was weak and barely audible. It was late in the day on the eighth of February, 1995. Park staff in the headquarters had gone home, but I was working late in another building. For some reason, I had left my hand-held radio on. I had known that Dick was ill. A week earlier when Leon and I had stopped in we found that he had not been hiking in over a week and was having difficulty keeping the cabin warm. We had chopped some wood for him and shoveled the pathway to the wood shed.

Dick was calling to say that he was very sick and needed help. Worse yet, it was one of those days when he had to snowshoe down to Low Pass in subzero temperatures to do so. I made some quick phone calls and within the hour, Port Alsworth pilot Mark Lang flew up to get Dick. After a night in town, Dick left Alaska to spend the remainder of the winter with his brother Raymond in California.

That was one of my final radio conversations with Dick. It marked the last winter that he would spend in his cabin, and later that year I relocated to the parks coastal field office in Kenai. Although I still spent time with him during the summer months, I no longer had the pleasure of turning on my radio in the morning and listening to the voice of my friend from Upper Lake.

Dick had a lifelong impact on me. Among his many attributes, those which stand tallest were his love of wilderness, his keen sense of observation, and his presence of mind to record what he saw. A diesel mechanic by trade, decades of living in the wilderness transformed Dick into a self-trained field naturalist. He was fascinated by weather phenomena, annual phenological events, cyclic natural fluctuations in animal populations, and predator-prey interactions.

He didn't visit an active Great-horned owl nest merely to photograph the birds, he persistently re-visited the nest to observe and record the onset and duration of incubation, the number and fate of owlets, and even examined prey remains in owl pellets below the nest. He didn't keep an eye on lake ice and snow cover merely to assure the safe landing of his mail planes, he systematically measured monthly winter snow pack and lake ice thickness to within a quarter of an inch, and did so with instruments that he made himself.

In *A Sand County Almanac* Aldo Leopold wrote: "Keeping records enhances the pleasure of the search, and the chance of finding order and meaning in these events." At Twin Lakes, Dick found pleasure in recording natural events. He wrote most of his notes on wall calendars, the type that rural Iowa hardware stores give to loyal customers at the start of the New Year. Entries included dates of lake freeze-up, lake ice break-up, den entry and den emergence by brown bears, first calving by moose, first lambing by Dall sheep, and nest initiation by gray jays. Dick had a special interest in wolves and kept close records of winter pack size, number of kills, and species of prey.

Dick's calendars and journals are among the longest continuous records for any Alaska national park. Trends in the duration of lake ice cover on Upper Twin Lake plotted from Dick's records (1969–95) parallel those of other Northern Hemisphere sites and provide evidence that freshwater ecosystems are responding to a warming climate. Dick's love for wilderness, passion for observing and understanding the natural world around him, and dedication to keeping records were an inspiration to many.

During the last year of Dick's life I was developing a long-term plan to monitor the physical and biological resources of Lake Clark National Park and Preserve and four of its sister park units in Southwest Alaska. After he passed away, I dedicated that monitoring plan to him.

Today the instruments that Dick used to measure the environment surrounding him at Upper Twin Lake stand idle in his cabin, or in the corner of his woodshed. Visitors occasionally pick one up to admire it. But a short distance to the west a remote automated weather station is recording air temperature, wind velocity, rainfall, snow depth, relative humidity, and solar radiation. Data is automatically transmitted hourly to regional and national climate centers. Nearby a camera equipped with a panoramic lens is taking a fixed-position photograph every day to record the timing and extent of snow cover. Overhead a satellite named MODIS is recording the date on which Upper and Lower Twin Lake freeze and the duration that ice remains on the lakes. I can't help but think that if Dick were still alive he would be on top of it all. And the questions? Boy, would he have the questions.

Don't just give it to them, they gotta work for it

John Erickson

I started flying in 1978, and after a season in Kodiak, Alaska I went back to Washington State where I flew floatplanes for many years. One day I ran into one of the owners of Alaska's Wilderness Lodge in Port Alsworth. He kept asking me, "Why don't you come fly for our lodge?" The more I learned about this fishing lodge, located on a picturesque point at the mouth of Hardenburg Bay on Lake Clark, the better it sounded. So in 1992 I headed back north to Alaska.

My first week on the job was in early June of 1992. After I had taken a few flights to get familiar with the local area the owners of the lodge said, "When you get a chance you need to go up and see Dick Proenneke." Our lodge guests arrived on Saturday and there was always time to kill that day because we didn't have any fishing trips set up. We issued fishing licenses, gave a brief introduction to the lodge, showed one of the Dick Proenneke videos, and had a Park Ranger give a presentation on Lake Clark National Park and Preserve. After seeing the Proenneke video a few of the lodge guests would come up to me bubbling with enthusiasm and asking, "Can we go up to see Dick?"

On my first visit, I loaded the guests into a floatplane and we took off for the thirty-minute flight to Upper Twin Lake. When we arrived at Dick's it was like stepping into the film we had just watched. Dick, standing on his beach, greeted us warmly. After exchanging introductions, he led us to his cabin and talked a mile-a-minute while my guests snapped pictures and asked questions whenever Dick stopped to take a breath. I sort of just stood back, watched, and listened. I soon realized that at Proenneke's cabin my role as "guide" ended once the floatplane was tied up.

Those visits to Twin Lakes would quickly become a routine for us, taking place almost every week. If the weather was not flyable on Saturday we would stop at Dick's on another day after we finished fishing or some guests were willing to forego fishing to see Dick. Our stops were always unannounced. We just showed up, and if he was there, Dick would give us a little tour of his place, explain his daily routine, and pose for pictures with the guests. He loved the picture sessions and knew exactly where he wanted everyone to stand to take advantage of the best sun angle. He always liked to have people get a picture of themselves looking out through the top of the Dutch door of his cabin. And we still do that today.

His "birds"—gray jays—were always part of the visit. If the jays hadn't already been drawn in by the sight and voices of lodge guests milling around the cabin, Dick would call them "Hey, guys, come on, you guys." Dick's jay calling is etched in my memory. When they came in he would pass out crackers and tell the guests, "Now hold the cracker tight. Don't just give it to them, they gotta work for it." He'd hold the cracker tightly in his hand and really make them peck and pry to pull it out of his hand. Some guests would be a little timid at the prospect of a screaming gray jay landing on them and they would just place the cracker in the palm of their hand. "No, oh no," Dick would quickly command, "you want to hold it tight, they got to work for a living."

If the weather were not threatening Dick would ask the group, "Does anybody want to go on a hike?" If we had the time and the guests were interested, Dick would usually take us up to his Teetering Rock, an angular 3-ton boulder. He would take charge of the group, hand everyone a walking stick from the many he kept neatly stacked behind his woodshed, and lead the group up the trail. Along the way he would often stop and point out things of interest, like bear-marked spruce trees and tundra plants. Dick seemed to always set a pace that matched the capabilities of the guests, some of whom might be overweight or elderly. When we reached the Teetering Rock, Dick explained how a glacier must have dropped it right on top of another rock buried in the soil. He then positioned himself alongside the rock and pushed to get it rocking. Once rocking he would say, "Now I want you all to listen, watch, and count how many times it rocks." I seem to remember that he once got it to rock thirty-two times!

Hiking to Teetering Rock took on another twist once the blueberries ripened in August. Dick would tell the group, "Let's go up and go grazing." As we hiked up toward Teetering Rock Dick demonstrated his technique for crawling along on the tundra while picking and eating blueberries, what he called "grazing for blueberries." I remember do-ing that a time or two with him. The guests thought it was fun, and like him, many found it easier to lie down to pick rather than bending over or trying to walk on their knees.

What I noticed quickly was Dick's ability to connect and communicate with not only me but with the guests. They would frequently ask Dick, "How do you do without this or that." And Dick would say, "Don't make life so complicated. Just simplify everything. If I need to wash my clothes, I just put 'em in the lake, let them soak for a few hours, some-times I use a little soap, sometimes I don't." His simple lifestyle always resonated with the guests, many of whom were taking a break from their complicated and stressful lives back home.

On many of our trips we brought Dick mail and food. We used to bring our lunches in a big canvas bag. After we'd all eaten lunch Dick would kind of take it upon himself to root through the bag. Finding something he wanted he'd ask, "Well, you gonna use anymore of this?" It was usually small packages of sugar or tea, but what really always caught his attention were the little Heinz ketchup packets. One day, after he had stuffed most of the remaining seven or eight packets of ketchup in his pocket—he would never take them all—I got curious and asked, "Dick, what will you use those for?" He replied, "They're like fresh greens." Puzzled, I asked, "What do you mean, fresh greens?" He said, "Oh, that's a carbohydrate, better than a box of raisins. When I want to go hiking I can just whip one of these things out and pop it open." From that time forward I told our cook to throw in some extra ketchup packets.

Over the years I made a trip to see Dick almost every week and took hundreds of lodge guests to his place. After a couple years we began to have repeat guests that would come back to the lodge every year. The first question many would ask was, "Is Dick still here?" I would take them back to visit Dick and he always seemed to remember them, especially those that had been corresponding with him. Dick treated all the visitors the same despite the fact that some had lofty credentials. One year the list of visitors I chauffeured included NFL Hall of Fame quarterback John Elway and Army General Norman Schwarzkopf, Chief of the U.S. Central Command. Dick was always receptive to having visitors, but one year I asked him, "Dick, do you not want us coming here?" He responded by saying that he loved meeting and talking to the people.

Because I was usually there with lodge guests we only hiked around the cabin or up to Teetering Rock. He did take me on one longer hike up Hope Creek and into what he called First Canyon. He was going to show me one of his favorite places that he named eye of the needle, a rock spire with a hole in it that could be seen after climbing up the north end of First Canyon. The day started out beautiful, but as we made our way in, the clouds crept down lower on the mountains and the wind really started blowing. Minutes later we were in fog and Dick said, "No. We aren't going any farther. Let's head on back down." Maybe that was a blessing because as I remember it I was physically spent trying to keep up with him. It wasn't that his pace was fast, he had a relatively slow pace. That made it harder for me because his steps were shorter. So it was almost like I had to do double duty, because it was the same distance but my stride was longer, and Dick was steady and relentless. Dick could walk you into the ground. If you didn't turn him off he just didn't stop. You had to say, "Dick, I need a break!"

* * *

All the years I knew Dick he traded or bartered for almost everything. One winter I heard that Dick was thinking about spending part of the winter in Port Alsworth. I offered him our house because I knew we were going to be gone for about a month and a half on a long vacation. Dick immediately said, "No, I can't do that." I responded by explaining to him that I was not just offering him a place to stay, but that we NEEDED somebody to watch the house for us because we were going to be gone. "Oh," he piped up, "well if you need somebody to housesit, I could do that." So my wife went out and got a bunch of fresh strawberries and cut and froze them and put some meat and other items in the refrigerator for Dick.

That's kind of the way Dick was. I think he didn't like to barter in the typical sense of the word. Glen and Lake Clark Air would go out and pick Dick up or take him his mail. They did it as a courtesy, but Dick would repay Glen by helping out, working on some of the tractors at The Farm Lodge and grading the runway.

His most sought-after contribution was the grading of the aircraft run-way in spring and fall. It was a "bush" runway that Babe Alsworth had carved from what the glaciers left behind. It was not entirely level, and during its early years lacked an essential ingredient: gravel. Grading it was a challenge that few besides Dick Proenneke would master. I have a vivid mental picture of him standing up there on that LeTour-neau grader going up and down the runway for hours on end.

One year when Dick was grading it, the grader started to veer off the north edge of the runway where it met Hardenburg Bay. The old LeTourneau didn't really have any brakes, and as it crossed over onto the slope leading to the bay it rolled down the hill and hit one of Glen's Cessna 206 floatplanes. It did some serious damage to the tail. Dick finally got the grader turned around, but he didn't even bat an eye. He didn't stop to look at the damaged plane, he just backed up and returned to grading the runway. After a while Laddie Elliot (Glen Als-worth's father-in-law) came out and asked what had happened. Dick hollered down from the grader, "I told Glen to buy the parts to fix these brakes fifteen years ago."

* * *

Dick had a really good sense of humor. After he had his first mild stroke and returned to Port Alsworth, I saw him as I was walking the road in front of the church. Dick was in his usual garb, with his hat, walking stick, and an old pair of Carhartts. I got up closer and his face was pulled off to one side and one eye was half clinched shut. My mind was racing, "Man, he looks messed up. That stroke really did him a number." I called out, "Hi, Dick. How's it going?"

He perked up and straightened his face out. His eyes had that same twinkle and seemed as bright as ever. He looked one-hundred per-cent normal. I said, "What are you doing?"

And he said, "Well, they told me I had a stroke so I thought I'd play the part."

* * *

During one of Dick's final years at Twin Lakes he hurt his back and I flew in to pick him up. The lake hadn't frozen yet, and Alaska's Wilderness Lodge had the only float plane available. When I arrived at Twin Lakes in the lodge's Cessna 206 the weather was horrible; it was about five degrees with a strong west wind. The only place I could land was up the lake from Carrithers's point, a mile from Dick's cabin. I had circled his cabin beforehand and saw Dick with his little backpack. Although we couldn't communicate, he knew the situation and was waving and motioning for me to go up lake to land.

Dick headed out as I circled a few more times. He had to break trail through a couple feet of snow. I successfully landed but the waves were pounding on the floats and the water was freezing instantly. Fortunately I didn't have to wait but a few minutes before Dick came popping out of the brush. The shoreline at this spot is armored with large rocks and they were covered with six inches of ice; it was like everything had been dipped in wax along the beach. I was standing in the water struggling to hold the plane away from the rocks and at the same time yelling at Dick, "Just get in the plane." Dick scrambled up over me, somehow managing to keep his footing on the ice-covered floats, and climbed into the plane. I pushed off from the beach, jumped into the cockpit, and started the engine. I back-taxied before I turned into the wind and poured on the power. We were airborne in seconds, and as we were putting on our seatbelts I said to Dick, "I thought your back was hurting."

Dick barked, "It is. It's killing me!" He was just plain tough.

It was not the first time that an emergency flight had to be launched to bring Dick out of Twin Lakes. Later I asked him if it was getting harder to stay out there alone at his cabin. Dick replied, "No, but there's a lot of people that are concerned about me." He admitted that he was an old guy but said he didn't want people to have to worry about him. He also knew that if something happened, the Park Service or someone else might have to come up there on a really bad weather day to help him out. Worse yet, something could happen during those times of the year where it's not possible to get to Proenneke's cabin with anything short of a helicopter. I remember talking to him about it and him saying, "I don't want to be a burden and have people worrying about me." It's easier, he said, if I just stay at my cabin in the summer but come out in the winter and live in Port Als-worth or with my brother, Raymond, in California.

Bush pilot and fishing guide John Erickson has been flying visitors to Twin Lakes for almost twenty-five years. Since 2012 he has worked for Operation Heal Our Patriots and flies wounded veterans in to see the Richard Proenneke site.

One Man's Wilderness should be left as it was

Jeanette Mills

On the last day of July in 1998, my husband Jerry, Chris Degernes and her dog Trapper and I began a hike that would take us from Telaquana Lake south to Twin Lakes. Jerry and I were Park Service volunteers stationed at Telaquana Lake. Chris had spent a good deal of time at Twin Lakes in the past and knew Dick Proenneke well. For Jerry and me, it would be our initial meeting, and one that we looked forward to for some time. We had heard so much about Dick and we knew that this could be his last summer at Twin Lakes.

Fog and a light mist greeted us on the day we reached the shore of Lower Twin Lake. Jana Walker, a seasonal Park Ranger, picked us up and we spent the evening at the nearby ranger cabin. Snow fell that night, followed by a mix of rain and snow the next morning. By four in the afternoon visibility improved and we were ready and eager to head up to see Dick Proenneke. "No go, too windy," said Dick over the Park Service radio. So we stayed put, and watched a group of thirty-eight Dall sheep across the lake on a slope below the snow line.

The next morning we got an early start at 6:30 a.m. The lake was still too rough to launch the Zodiac, so we planned to hike to the Upper Lake to see Dick. We no sooner had started out when Dick called on the radio to say the wind was lying down by his place, so we turned around and hiked back to get the boat. It was a cold ride but when we arrived at the Upper Lake it was indeed calmer, just as Dick had said.

Dick greeted us when we reached his beach and we visited for a bit, during which he invited us for supper. Chris had permission for us to stay in a nearby cabin so we left to get settled in, but really, to give Dick a chance to rest since he was recovering from a cold. Of course Dick wouldn't say that he needed the rest but we all knew he did.

When we returned to Dick's cabin I learned about hot Tang and how good it is on a cool gray day. Hot Tang was also one of Dick's home remedies. When the cookie and Tang break was over we got busy with making supper. Visitors staying across the lake had given Dick two small lake trout, which he filleted lickity-split. While watching him I was thinking he could have done it with his eyes closed, given the number of fish he must have filleted over the years.

Chris and Jerry came in from splitting wood about the time Dick finished frying the fish. We all sat around the wood stove on impromptu seats, doorsill, stool, and rounds of wood. Dick had also fried up the lake trout heads and asked, "Who wants one?" Chris and I said we would pass on that offer. I couldn't get past eating the eyeballs. Jerry said he would try one. Dick took the other head, then grabbed some ketchup, proclaiming "everything tastes better with ketchup." Jerry reported afterward that there was not much taste, other than that of ketchup, but the head required a lot of chewing.

I remember while we were eating I asked a question about his ewe Dall sheep skull above the fireplace. I meant to find out what the story was behind it; instead I ended up asking something really dumb— "what was it?" I know I flushed red in the face and didn't correct myself as I should have, but Dick just answered my question. I pretty much kept my mouth shut after that, except when we talked about Shuyak Island where Dick, like us, had spent some time during his years on Kodiak.

I couldn't help but feel nervous around Dick, because here was this man that seemed to know EVERYTHING and I knew less than a thimbleful about wilderness living at that time. But Dick never made me feel like the greenhorn that I truly was. In fact, he was just the opposite, full of questions about Telaquana Lake, what wildlife we had seen, and our plans for winter caretaking.

We learned about Buhach from Dick that evening. Buhach is a mosquito repellent in the form of a powder that when burned produces smoke. Dick liked to keep the upper half of his Dutch door open to bring more light into his cabin and he had some burning during supper to discourage the bugs from joining us. I found it rather noxious, and later we wondered if it was healthy for Dick to burn that stuff inside his cabin.

Dick told us all about the bull moose that was killed down by Low Pass beach the previous winter. He figured it was a seven- or eight-year-old. The antler spread measured just over fifty-nine inches, with three brow tines on one side and four on the other. But what was most impressive was the number of points—fifteen on one side and sixteen on the other. This moose died in the prime of his life. Dick could only guess at how it died because he wasn't living in his cabin that winter.

Our conversation turned to how that was a good way to go—in the prime of your life. "No fun getting old and frail, unable to hike in the mountains, and be reminded daily of all you can't do anymore," said Dick. None of us could imagine Dick looking forward to life in California after such a great run at Twin Lakes.

After supper Dick was in the mood for giving gifts, probably because he knew he wasn't coming back. He gave Jerry his famous tin-crimping tool that he used to make trays from discarded fuel cans. Chris received a very cool stick of diamond willow that I knew she would cherish even if she didn't carve it into anything. I got a berry picker that Dick had found at the head of the lake. It was made mostly of wood, except for the metal tines. Dick didn't know who had left it up there, just one of the many things he had found on his hikes that was too good not to keep. Dick said he wished he could give his hand-made tin one to me, but that it should stay with the cabin. Dick said that "One Man's Wilderness" should be left as it was.

I remember the overall mood was solemn that evening, although we all tried not to think of it as the end. To imagine your life and belongings becoming a museum can't be a pleasant thought. But perhaps Dick knew that people would be happy to see his cabin as it was back in the days when he lived there.

People came by Dick's cabin quite often while we were there. We took a walk up to Teetering Rock with Dick and two park visitors tagging along. Across from Hope Creek we saw two Dall sheep ewes, one with that year's lamb. A floatplane brought in a party of four to camp at Hope Creek for four or five days. Four people staying at Windsong Lodge also boated over. So although it was still "One Man's Wilderness," it was becoming a busy place.

I remember Dick's rock collection on the west side of his cabin and a rock with a thin pink covering on most of it. "What did we think that was?" he asked. Jerry looked closely and said it looked like some type of glue or goop. Indeed that is what it was. Dick had found it somewhere around the lake. At first look he too wondered what it could be, then he realized it was manmade rock art. He brought it back to his cabin not only to clean up after someone, but also as a way to question people about it. Dick loved to ask you questions—make you think!

Dick asked us about Dick Straty's cabin, which is at the upper end of Telaquana Lake. Straty started his log cabin at Telaquana Lake about the same time as Dick did at Upper Twin, although neither knew each other was doing so at the time. Straty lived in Juneau and used his cabin seasonally, especially during the hunting season. The two would later become friends and visit each fall when Straty (a pilot) stopped at Upper Twin to see Dick. One thing they used to tease each other about was whose cache would fall over first. Now that both have passed on they will never know, but to their credit both caches are still standing proud and straight.

Our last day with Dick was going to include a hike to Low Pass but it was raining. Two bull caribou walked by on his beach that morning. Chris caught a flight out with Alaska West's Otter floatplane. It would be a luxurious ride because they had dropped off hunters out west and she was their only passenger on the return flight. We said our goodbyes to Dick and climbed into the boat for the ride back down to the lower lake ranger cabin. When we left, Dick was busy with a group of visitors that came over from Hope Creek to meet him.

* * *

I can't remember exactly how it came to be that I would undertake the long process of transcribing Dick's journals, which by accounts weighed close to one hundred pounds. It wasn't until after Dick had left Upper Twin Lake that we wrote back and forth about his dream to see a book in his OWN WORDS created from his journals. He felt bad that author Sam Keith had put "words in his mouth" when he produced *One Man's Wilderness*. This time he wanted his daily account of life at Twin Lakes to be told in his own words. He wanted to see the book in his lifetime, but sadly that didn't happen. Two volumes of Dick's journals have been published and a third will be released next year. I look forward to the time when Dick's words will be available for all to read.

Because I transcribed his journals many people automatically assume that I am a "Dick Proenneke expert." Of course I can recall many facts from the transcription work, but there are also many more that I've forgotten. Dick felled the trees for his cabin the year that I was born. Toward the end of Dick's life, I was nothing more than a visitor who turned into a frequent correspondent after he moved to Hemet, California. Dick enjoyed the wilderness stories I wrote about in my letters, as they no doubt reminded him of his younger days at Twin Lakes.

Dick was by far the most personable "bush rat" I have ever met. He was genuine in his like and curiosity about people. He would have made a great instructor because he sure knew how stimulate everyone's imagination, make them think, and want to learn more!

In May 1994 Jeanette left Minneapolis, Minnesota with a couple of duffle bags and headed for Alaska. Her new life began during the winter of 1995 after she met Jerry. Together they have called Telaquana Lake home since 1997, working as Volunteers for Lake Clark National Park and Preserve.

I think it's time for a kiss

Sandy Lang

"December 26 1978. Overcast, calm and 16 degrees. Mail, a batch of it. Later I counted more than 75 cards and letters and fourteen packages if you count big fat padded envelopes as packages. A couple packages I mailed had come back for more postage. I asked Glen (Alsworth) about the radical postage fee of $2.20 on a 6 oz. 4th class package. Something wrong there and he agreed. His guess was that Pat (Alsworth) had weighed a heavy one or two and a light one and put the heavy postage on the light package!" RLP

I was the U.S. Postmaster in Port Alsworth for thirty years. During that time I got to know everybody really well. Mail takes on special significance in a small Alaskan bush community, and I always tried to take good care of the residents and their letters. Dick Proenneke was one of my customers, and, I should say, one of my best customers. I always made sure that the mail was handled properly for him because mail was very, very important to him.

One day I was sorting the mail when I came across a rather blank looking envelope. All it had written on it was "R. L. P. 99653." At the time, I wondered, who in the world is that. And then it dawned upon me, "Richard L. Proenneke." When I personally delivered that letter to Dick he thought it was pretty funny because I figured out exactly who those initials belonged to. I said, "Dick, everybody knows who you are." And he just laughed.

Dick loved to hike, and one winter that he spent in Port Alsworth he and I hiked almost every day. After the post office closed he'd come to the door and say, "Okay. Are you ready to go?" And then he'd take our dogs—Nubbins, Jenny, and later Corky, our little Australian terrier—and me and off we'd go off on the two-mile hike to the waterfall (Tanalian Falls).

It was pretty interesting doing that because the dogs would run twice as much as we would walk, but not the little terrier Corky. As time went on, she became slower and slower, and pretty soon she'd just call it quits, turn around, and go home. Dick would always call her "the little wimp" because she wouldn't go all the way to the falls with us.

On one of our first hikes we got all the way to the top of a steep hill and stopped for a little bit of a rest. As we stood there Dick said, "Well, Sandy. I think it's time for a kiss."

I looked at him, both surprised and puzzled, thinking, "What! What in the world is going on?" And then he broke into that funny little smile, dug into his pocket, and pulled out a chocolate candy kiss.

Hiking with Dick was never dull. He was like the pied piper traveling with all of his little animal friends, and we had a great time walking together and just talking and sharing various stories and experiences. Many times it was pretty slippery walking, and I remember going down one particularly steep hill arm-in-arm, and he always would say, "Well, I sure like hiking with you because you hike the same exact stride as I do." He said, "A lot of people I walk with walk way too fast or too slow, but you're just right." So it always made me feel special that he enjoyed walking with me.

Because Dick had a reputation for wearing out footwear it was always interesting to see what he had on his feet. I remember one time Dick came over to our house and he was wearing these intriguing shoes. They resembled rubber slip-ons, and shoes similar to what Dick was wearing are being manufactured today.

My husband, Mark, asked, "Dick, where did you get those shoes?"

Dick replied, "Oh, they used to be hip boots."

 "What!" said Mark.

Dick turned to Mark and explained, "Yeah, after the hip boots got a hole on the top I cut the upper half off. Then I had knee boots for a while. But then as time went on I kept cutting them down. I stopped cutting when they were just below my ankles. So now these are my house slippers. That's what I call them. You can't waste anything. The rubber was still good on that part, so I figured I might as well just keep trimming them down until there was nothing left of them."

* * *

Many years ago we needed to build a driveway from the east end of the south aircraft runway to where our house sits today. It meant installing a culvert over a creek that feeds into Hardenburg Bay. We asked Dick if he would help us because he used to be a cat skinner. With no hesitation he agreed to do the work. Dick ran the dozer and took charge while Mark and a friend, Bill Schmitz, did the hand work with shovels.

If Mark and Bill didn't already know it, they were quickly reminded that Dick worked at one pace—full speed and nonstop. Dick put the culvert in and then began building up the road with gravel. Dick was constantly getting after them to do this and do that. At one point Mark and Bill stopped working to take a little rest. As he went by on the dozer Dick looked down and called out, "You know, you're not going to get too much work done leaning on those shovels."

Mark and Bill were worn out at the end of the day, but when the project was finished it was perfect. The driveway came out beautifully and the big front lawn that we have today was a result of Dick straightening out a road that was haphazardly built years earlier when the runway was extended.

When he was finished with our driveway we asked Dick what we owed him for all his hard work. He said, "Oh, I don't want to be paid in cash or anything like that." But then he added, "Probably a couple of gold coins would be good."

We thought for a moment. Was he serious, gold coins? We went to a bank and purchased a few gold coins to pay him with, but I don't know what he ever did with them. I think they were worth a hundred dollars each at the time. We knew Dick liked gold nuggets, but it was kind of interesting that he also liked gold coins!

* * *

One winter Dick was dog sitting for our neighbors, Ed and Cathy Painter. He seemed to really like their dog. One day he came over to visit and after we had talked for a while he dug into one of his shirt pockets, pulled out a doggy bone and said, "Sandy, I need you to do something for me."

I said, "Sure. What is that?"

He said, "You know that grinder thing that you have in your house?"

And I said, "You mean my Cuisinart?"

"Yeah, yeah. That's it." He said, "I want you to grind this up for me and make it small. I tried soaking it but that didn't do anything so I want you to grind it up."

Astonished, I said, "Dick. This is a dog bone. You know it's a treat that you give a dog when they obey your command?"

He said, "I know, but I've been reading on the box and it's full of all kinds of healthy sounding things and it even has a breath mint at the end." He said, "I think that would be something really good, don't you?"

I said, "Dick, There is no way I'm grinding up a dog bone for you to eat."

"Well, I don't see anything wrong with it. I just wanted to eat it for breakfast."

My final words were, "You're not going to be eating dog bones."

After Dick left Alaska and went to live with his brother he and I would correspond. He always told me how excited he was to get letters from me and find out all the news about our dogs and people in the community. I've saved many of the letters he wrote me and they will always be very, very special because he was such a close friend and somebody that I really admired and appreciated. I certainly do miss him; he was just a good buddy.

Sandy and Mark Lang have lived in Port Alsworth since 1976. At that time they worked for a fishing lodge (Fishing Unlimited) and took clients to Twin Lakes to meet Dick Proenneke. Later they built Lake Clark Inn, which they owned, and operated for many years. Mark and Sandy now manage Samaritan Lodge Alaska for Operation Heal Our Patriots.

Can I borrow these to make a copy

Alan Bennett

Most people write notes on their wall calendars; grandchildren's birthdays, anniversaries, dental appointments, and vacations. Dick Proenneke wrote on wall calendars too, but day by day, month by month, over the course of a year, his calendars were more like chapters of a book, complete with illustrations. He began making notes on wall calendars in 1968 and did so almost every year that he lived at Upper Twin Lake. The calendars were not fancy; they were the free promotional versions given away by merchants, restaurants, and banks each year around Christmas. They usually measured 8x11 ½ inches and were gridded into one-and-a-quarter-inch squares. Many were from Iowa and sent to him by his family.

I became fascinated with Dick's calendars from the first time I saw them. The current year's calendar usually hung on the wall to the right of his desk. He kept all the older calendars neatly stored away in boxes arranged by year. The most recent years were kept in a box under the left side of his desk and within easy reach. The older calendars were kept in a larger box and stored under his lower bunk. At first Dick seemed a bit puzzled by my interest in his old calendars, perhaps because I was the first to ask about them. One cold winter day he pulled them all out for me to look at. To a biologist, decades of notes on plants, animals, and weather conditions in a remote unstudied area of Alaska was the information-equivalent of a Golden Fleece. No such information existed for any other spot within the four million-acre Park and Preserve.

After a long exchange of questions and answers, I finally asked, "Can I borrow these to make a copy? I'll bring them right back." Dick did not immediately answer. Finally, and with what I sensed was some reluctance, he replied, "Sure, but not this year's."

Aside from my interest in the information contained on the calendars, I was concerned about their fate. Writing on some was done in pen, and over the years moisture had caused the ink to bleed. Notes written in pencil had steadily faded and some were becoming illegible. A few calendars were developing the texture of well-worn dishtowels from years of storage and handling. They all had that smoky aroma of Dick's cabin. I took the calendars to Port Alsworth, where month-by-month I photocopied twenty-three years' worth, a very slow process.

The notes that Dick entered on his calendars were simple at first but grew in complexity each year as he added more symbols, illustrations, and an ever-increasing range of information. Those familiar with both Dick's journals and calendars have recognized a pattern. The older he grew, the less he would write in journals and the more he would write on calendars. Age may have played some role in this, but I think the principle reason was that over time Dick came to value the calendars for their convenience of past and present comparisons. Did the lake ice go out earlier this year than last? When was the last

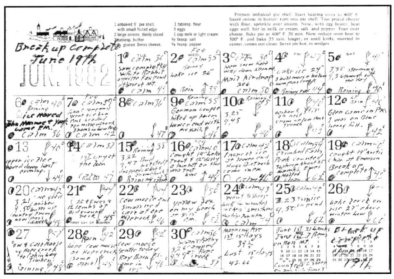

winter that the snow pack was over forty inches? Is this the earliest I've seen a robin in spring? Paging thorough his calendars would answer his questions much quicker than wading through his journals.

On his very first calendars, 1968-69, Dick recorded the daily high and low temperatures in degrees Fahrenheit, made a small sketch of the moon to indicate its quarterly phase, and placed an "X" on each day to mark its passing. Sadly, his calendars from 1970-72 are missing, so the timing of any additions that he might have made during those years will remain a mystery. At some time during those three years he stopped making the daily checkmarks and began recording days with rain, snow, or fog. But he did not record precipitation amounts until 1974. His sketches of moon phase were short-lived because on future calendars they were pre-printed by the publisher. In 1975 he recorded lake ice thickness (in inches) at his "water hole" offshore from his cabin. He recorded ice thickness at random intervals but usually at least once every ten days. Remarkably, the ice on Upper Twin Lake was twenty-five-and- a-half inches thick on Memorial Day of that year.

On September 5, 1975 he began to record sky conditions, wind direction and wind speed. Degree of cloud cover was indicated on a small circle. An empty circle meant skies were clear, and a shaded circle indicated overcast conditions corresponding to the proportion of the circle shaded. He used an upward arrow to indicate a west (up lake) wind and a downward arrow to indicate an east (down lake) wind. He placed horizontal bars on the shaft of the arrow to indicate wind velocity in 10-mph increments. An arrow with no bars meant a wind less than 10 mph. Wind speed and direction were recorded twice daily with upper and lower arrows for morning and afternoon, respectively. Interestingly, wind was not recorded in 1976, but as those of us who have visited Twin Lakes know, it probably wasn't for lack of wind. 1976 was also the first year that he recorded the date on which Upper Twin Lake became ice-free, June 9.

Dick began recording wind speed using the Beaufort scale (a numerical rating of wind speed from 0 to 8) on his calendars after 1977, but he still used the arrows and bars for several more years. The first phenological events began to appear on his calendars in 1978-79. He recorded first sighting of robins, moose calves, Dall sheep lambs, and bear cubs. He also began recording freeze-up and break-up dates for both lakes and computed average temperature for the first and last half of each month. Fifteen-day averages were entered in a blank space before the first or last day of the month and in later years on the top of the calendars.

In 1980, Dick's calendars took a major turn. He began to add a wide range of phenological information spanning the entire year, including first arrival dates for migratory birds, nest initiation, and hatch dates for owls and song-birds, as well as blooming dates for plants and first sightings of red salmon. Dick kept a close eye on the sun. He added small drawings to illustrate the alignment of the sun with the mountain peaks to the south. A sketch on July 17 at 8:25 am places the sun squarely above the peak of Crag Mountain and another on October 5th at 12:00 noon places the sun directly above the peak of Cowgill Mountain. The perspective of the drawings corresponds closely to what you would see if you were standing in front of his cabin. Over the next couple of years Dick's drawings would illustrate the sun/mountain peak alignments with respect to date and time for all the mountain peaks on both sides of the two lakes.

Another major change in the calendars occurred during the summer of 1982 when Dick began entering his daily activities. "Wrote letters, cooked beans, hauled wood, picked berries, sharpened saws, did laundry, improved ice auger and snowshoe bindings." He also added daily hiking destinations and more detail on his visitors and what they did while at Twin Lakes. The calendars began to become more cluttered and to "highlight" entries that he deemed most important he used a felt-tipped pen. Entries that warranted such highlighting included a lake ice depth of 41.5 inches on May 9 and lake breakup date of June 19.

Daily activities dominated the daily entries during 1983 and 1984. Weather observations, which had been the hallmark of his calendars during the 1970s, became intermittent, and on some days were not mentioned at all. Legibility began to suffer as Dick squeezed ever more information into a small space. Monthly weather summaries, which now included snowfall, snow pack, and ice depth, were written across the top of the calendars. If there were more to add after the day's entries had exhausted all the available space, he would write a "second layer" of information vertically. The names of visitors would usually be written in bold over the top of his daily activity notes.

The content of Dick's entries shifted again in 1985-86. He described weather conditions in great detail but seldom mentioned his routine daily activities. Comparing 1984 and 1985 on January 14th, days with similar weather, illustrates the contrast. In 1984 he writes, "*baked bread, repaired mitts, wrote letters, hauled wood;*" whereas in 1985 his calendar reads, "*lowering ceiling and light snow, clearing in PM with snow on mts across, clear after sunset and lowering temp.*"

Dick's 1988-93 calendars were the most laden with information. He added barometric pressure to his daily entries in small print perpendicular to the other text. He managed to enter as many as twelve lines of text in just over one square inch of space! Whatever noteworthy Information wouldn't fit in the day's box, he added as a footnote on the bottom or side of the page. As someone who has spent many long hours staring at them I can say with certainty that there are abbreviations and symbols lurking on some calendars that only he can translate.

Some years there was more to make note of at Twin Lakes than others. One such year was 1989 when Dick wrote: "*January 21st, lowest barometer reading ever, 26.85; January 31; cold record for Twin Lakes, 5 days below –50 degrees; February 9, a first for Twin Lakes; two large coyotes came up lake and passed 175 yards out, thought they were wolves but tracks too small; April 25, dental appointment to get two front teeth rebuilt by Dr. Wright; August 8, strong winds and heavy overcast, two young German couples came down lake in inflatable canoes heading for Chili and Dillingham; Nov 15, wind changed direction 6 times; Dec 16, Redoubt (volcano) erupting, climbed Falls Peak, ash on the snow very noticeable in tracks, rabbit had crossed lake.*"

During 1996-97, Dick wrote in his journals but did not write on calendars. I may have had a role in this. After I took such an enthusiastic interest in his weather records and told him how valuable they might be in tracking climate change, Dick began a new system of record keeping. He reused the envelopes that his longevity bonus checks arrived in to create a "weather data sheet," (the Alaska Longevity Bonus Program which ended in 1997 provided Alaskans 65 and older with monthly checks of $250). After he had filled in the months' weather records he would send the envelopes to me in his outgoing mail. Although he entered the same weather observations in his journals, he may have considered the data sheets a replacement for the calendars those two years.

Dick made notes on what would be his last calendar during the summer months of 1998; his final extended stay at Twin Lakes. He did not write a journal that year. While it was Dick's journals and films that would make him famous, his calendars were a complement to both. If his annual journal were likened to a ball game, the corresponding calendar would be the highlight film. A quick glance at any month would usually reveal aircraft landings, names of visitors, his hiking destinations, important wildlife sightings, weather summary and storm events. Even more information would jump off the page if you knew where to look or used a hand lens to do so.

Dick wrote on calendars to create records for himself, and I think he enjoyed doing so. Over time those records helped him put his many years at Twin Lakes into perspective and enriched his understanding of the ecological drama and cycle of natural events that he witnessed. As his journal writing slowed and eventually stopped, he continued to write on his calendar. In many ways the two are linked. The next time you read Dick's journals and you bump into his words, "*strong wind blowing down lake this morning, fog and rain, good day to finally catch up on my journal*," imagine that he is sitting at his desk and occasionally glancing up at that calendar hanging from the wall. Notes that he made on it the previous day or the day before that refreshed his memory of what had happened while he was on a long day hike or too busy to open his journal.

Only a person of extraordinary stamina and personal drive could have lived Dick's life

Monroe Robinson

Dick Proenneke's cabin, cache, snow shovel, and every other hand-crafted item that made up his life at Twin Lakes reveal how he worked—his level of craftsmanship and how his work fit in with the life he chose to live. Dick had a remarkable natural sense of design and proportion. There are no overly heavy logs or poles in any of Dick's work. Everything from his cabin to hand-carved spoons are made just heavy enough to be structurally adequate for the job it was meant to do: not too heavy, not too light.

Looking closely at Dick's life, one becomes aware that Dick preferred to repair items rather than replace them. There are repairs to his old boots and repairs over the repairs, and the same is true of his snow shovel. He repaired his socks, his pants, and his ice crampons. Dick even repaired his walking sticks, which would have been more easily replaced, because I think repairing matched his philosophy more than making something new.

Dick Proenneke had extraordinary hand-eye coordination. This is most easily seen in the construction of his tables, chairs, and saw-horse. Using an auger bit fitted into his handmade handle, Dick drilled mortise holes into the bottom of a tabletop or chair seat. By rotating the handle with a little downward pressure, the sharpened bit would self-feed into the wood. These mortise holes received the fitted ends of spruce poles to make legs for his chairs, stools, tables, and sawhorse. Drilling one hole for a leg is not a difficult process. However, drilling four holes into the bottom of a tabletop or chair seat that lies upside-down on the ground is a different matter. To make the table look symmetrical Dick drilled all four legs into the bottom of the tabletop at exactly the same angle, with no guide other than his excellent hand-eye coordination. With innate intuition, Dick drilled those mortise holes symmetrically. The legs do not splay out awkwardly, nor are they too straight, which would give the table a stilted appearance. On Dick's desk chair the back legs angle back a few degrees more than the front legs tilt forward but all four legs tilt outward at the identical angle. All this makes for a beautiful and comfortable chair.

* * *

I met Dick Proenneke in 1982 when I hiked with John Branson from Telaquana Lake to Lake Clark with the purpose of meeting Dick as I traveled through the wilderness he called home. Every few years after meeting Dick I would write him and each time he would send a long descriptive letter of his life and wildlife observations at Twin Lakes.

When Dick Proenneke did not return to his cabin in 2000, Lake Clark National Park Historian John Branson asked me to come to Twin Lakes to consult with the park on stabilization and restoration of Dick's cabin. John knew my log work from helping me on a trussed log bridge and additions at Jay and Bella Hammond's homestead on Lake Clark. Knowing Proenneke's high regard for my work, John thought I would be Dick's choice.

I wasted no time getting started. Decades of rain, ice, and overflow from snow melt had not been kind to Dick's construction; the sill (bottom) logs on his cabin as well as those on the woodshed/ outhouse were rotted, as were the legs of his cache where they were buried in the ground. All the exposed timbers on the roofs of all three structures were rotted. I replaced rotted roof logs/poles in 2000 and the rotted sill logs and cache legs in 2003. I am still impressed with how tight Dick's cabin is, through the combination of his scribed log joints and the seal imparted by the oakum chinking between the logs.

For their protection, we moved many of Dick's most treasured handcrafted items to the park archives in 2000. All of Dick's outdoor handcrafted items, such as his sawhorse and beach chair, were losing integrity after years of exposure to the elements. Once restored, these too were moved to the archives. Each summer I replicated several of Proenneke's handcrafted items to have on display at his cabin, my goal being to keep the spirit and craft of Dick Proenneke intact for visitors who have come so far. I put all my skill and patience into this work, leaving none of me and take nothing of Dick's spirit away.

The best illustration of this was my replication of Dick's snow shovel which he made from the side of a fifteen-gallon steel drum with a spruce pole handle in 1967. He used this shovel for more than thirty years, and when it acquired a branching eleven-inch-long metal fatigue crack, Dick made a splint to span the crack. When the splint failed he replaced it.

Dick certainly had the skill to execute his work at whatever level of craftsmanship he desired. Dick constructed some of his smaller items during the summer of 1967, when his intent was to return the following year to build his cabin. As a practical man, his goal in 1968 was to construct his cabin, wood shed, and all the furniture he would need before winter. To complete all of this in one season he built everything with an efficiency, beauty, and creativity few would have the energy and skill to match.

Dick's philosophy was to live his life making all he needed, using no power tools and only materials he had close at hand. For Dick this was to experience life to its fullest. The only wood useful for carpentry at Twin Lakes is white spruce. Dick used white spruce to construct his cabin and cache logs, as well as his window sills and frames, his cabin door, the door hinges, door lock, all of his furniture, numerous beautiful spoons and a light weight and useful winter sled for hauling loads of firewood.

Dick kept the wilderness of Twin Lakes free of trash left by others. He referred to this as "tidying up". While 'tidying up' he would find thin sheet metal five-gallon aviation gas cans discarded by pilots. This became the metal Dick used. Using a pair of tin snips, he fabricated a hundred things, including his bread baking pans, skillet lids, storage containers, many pairs of hinges, and a warming oven on the side of his stove. Heavier metal came from larger oil and gas drums left around the lake. From these Dick made his snow shovel and ice crampons. Little went to waste. Dick salvaged metal from crashed airplanes. His anvil was part of the landing gear of a crashed Cessna 180. Salvaged aircraft sheet metal screws, bolts and nuts became useful when constructing his snow shovel and many other essential items.

Visitors to Dick Proenneke's cabin are most aware of the log work displayed in his cabin and cache, his sawn boards for the cabin door, and the wooden hinges. But Dick was equally accomplished working with metal; he even made his own crimping tool for crimping the edges of many sheet-metal objects. As with everything he constructed of wood, his metal work shows the same simplicity of functional design while not being overly heavy.

Many visitors to Dick's cabin will in some way make a comment about him writing lengthy letters to hundreds of people or cutting firewood by hand, commenting that "well of course, he had to do something with all his time" or "it probably kept him from being bored." Dick's life is so far removed from the life that most of us live that we have difficulty understanding that for Dick there was no "extra time" or time "getting bored."

Almost everything Dick built he completed in 1967 and 1968, and, in 1969, his cache. He then stopped building. Most craftsmen have an innate desire to keep building and building but Dick lived his philosophy of not endlessly creating more. Once his needs were met he had more time to pursue his other passions: hiking, observing wildlife, photography, filming, and writing journal entries and letters. Of course he still had to keep up with all the chores that living without power tools, appliances or electricity requires. Only a person of extraordinary stamina and personal drive could have lived Dick's life.

Along with the good fortune of walking in Dick's footsteps, it was at his cabin in 2000 that I met my soul mate, Kathryn Schubeck. Thereafter, the two of us would return year after year to care for Dick's cabin and greet an ever increasing number of visitors—visitors who travel from every corner of the globe to see this cabin for themselves. Kay and I have become keepers of the stories visitors tell of Proenneke's Twin Lakes. Every summer we are touched by those who weep or become overwhelmed and have a hard time speaking of the many ways Dick's story touched their dreams.

Occasionally, but rarely, the right person comes along at exactly the right time. That's what happened when Monroe Robinson arrived at Twin Lakes in 2000. Old unoccupied log cabins have a way of deteriorating fast, and uninvited bears are rough on wooden furniture. Monroe's timely restoration of Dick's cabin and his replication of Dick's creations, snow shovel to sled, have been a gift to us all. If that weren't enough, Monroe and his and wife, Kay Schubeck, have served as volunteer interpretive guides at the Richard Proenneke Site for over fifteen years.

I was trying to slide down the mountain but something stopped me

Jana Walker

"Tues, Sept 22. The season is closing fast. Very mild when Leon (Alsworth) stopped to pick me up at my cabin on upper Twin. – a good flight to Port Alsworth. Will I be back at Upper Twin in 99 and will Jana be Lower Lake Ranger? I feel sure she will be, in fact I bet her $25.00 that she will be. 1998 season was a very good one."
RLP

It was a smooth motorboat ride up to the head of Lower Twin Lake. I pulled the boat onto a sandy beach at the mouth of the stream connecting the upper and lower lakes. It was early June and the start of my initial summer stay at Twin Lakes as a seasonal Park Service ranger. One of my first orders of business was to go up and introduce myself to my neighbor, Dick Proenneke.

Before going any further, I called Dick on my hand-held radio to ask whether he thought the water was high enough to motor up the connecting stream. "Lake at twenty-five inches and too low to motor up the stream, you're going have to line that boat up," said Dick. I tried "long lining" the boat but quickly determined that I was no match for the connecting stream. I beached the boat and called Dick to say I was heading up on foot.

Meanwhile Dick launched his canoe and headed down lake. Less than an hour later we met each other about a third of the way up to his cabin. Dick recognized me but then, other than him, I was the only other soul within twenty miles of Twin Lakes on that day. He pulled into the beach, said "Hop aboard," and we set off toward his cabin. Along the way we stopped at a gravely beach edged with purple Jacob's ladder and shared some fruit cake while Dick quizzed me on my background and interests. Our final stop was his beach, where we pulled ashore and walked up to his cabin.

I'd watched the video of Dick building that cabin and had read *One Man's Wilderness,* with its priceless photographs of Dick's construction. Both the cabin and Dick had aged in those thirty years. He was eighty-two now, a little bent over, but still with a good supply of energy. During our afternoon chat it came out that he was ready to go to the "other side of the mountain" anytime. Reaching his 80th birthday was fine, but he didn't want to see five or ten more birthdays. He said he had done all he wanted to do with his life and was content.

After touring his cabin we ate lunch. He fixed me his specialty, sourdough hot cakes with peanut butter, honey, and onions! After lunch we walked up the beach to Carrithers's Point and looked at Hope's, Spike's, and Weisser's cabins, where Dick stored some of his belongings and where he occasionally put up overnight guests.

On the return to his place Dick took me on his "timberline trail" and talked about how he constructed it and placed blaze marks on some of the trees. Along the way he showed me his "big spruce" (a stout black spruce that was cored in 2009 and found to be over two hundred and thirty years old).

During our walk together the wind picked up and the lake was very rough and in no shape for Dick to take me back in his canoe. I would have to hike. He gave me instructions on how to make my way.

"See that deformed spruce out there?" he asked.

"Ah, I think so," was my response.

"There's driftwood lying on the trail to mark the spot to move off the shore," said Dick.

To me all the spruce looked deformed, but I nodded my head. We said our goodbyes and agreed that I'd call once I reached home. Off I went. I didn't find the driftwood trail, but I eventually found myself back at the beach fringed with Jacob's Ladder. Farther on, the lake eventually pushed me off the beach and uphill, where I found a game trail that led me past Dick's "Blueberry Hill" and eventually to the bluffs on the south shore. I launched the boat and rode a tailwind and whitecaps back to my ranger cabin.

One day during our morning radio chat a couple of weeks later Dick and I decided it would be a good day to hike up Emerson Creek. I'd been looking forward to that hike so I filled my backpack with extra clothing and food and climbed into the boat. The lake was like glass and I motored right up the center. When I reached the head of the lower lake I transferred my gear into the kayak that I had stationed there days earlier. I lined the kayak up the connecting stream, paying close attention. I wanted to study the stream and try to create a mental map of the deep sections should I work up the courage to try motoring upstream on the next trip.

When I reached the Upper Lake Dick was waiting. He led the way up the west side of the creek through an attractive quaking aspen forest, although full of mosquitoes. We went by the site of an old cabin that had burned the previous summer. Dick showed me the trail he has used over the years and maintained. The trail alternated between the woods and the gravel floodplain of the creek. About a mile upstream the peace and tranquility was briefly shattered by the noisy "cack, cack, cack" of a northern goshawk objecting to our presence near its nest. In classical goshawk fashion it swooped down, coming within a few feet of Dick's head. Dick laughed, and I could tell it wasn't the first time those two had met.

We scrambled over some loose rock and were rewarded with a view of Emerson Creek's lower waterfall. The rocky outcrop was brilliant green. There weren't many bugs and we had a beautiful view of the falls. From there we scrambled up a narrow, steep rock ledge and made our way toward the upper falls of Emerson Creek. I had to watch my footing and I worried about Dick and his mobility. It was rough terrain for an eighty-two year-old. He allowed me to give him a hand once and said, "My balance is a little off these days—especially at night."

I was amazed at the tremendous memory he had for the trails and land marks in this vast area. I've had neighbors in the city who knew less about their own backyards. We slowly made it up to a bluff, which gave us a panoramic view of the Emerson Creek Valley above us and the falls and streambed below us.

The sun gave way to some clouds and we agreed it was time to head back to the lake. Dick stopped along the way and pointed out the large rock in the stream with over two hundred layers. On an earlier trip he'd sat and counted them. "Of course, there might not be that many now. More of the rock could be covered up," he said.

When we reached his canoe we were greeted by a gusty east wind and the lake that was glassy calm while we were eating our lunch was now boiling with whitecaps. Dick had his trusty "gas paddle" (a 4-hp Sears outboard motor) lying in the bottom of his canoe. "Good time for the kicker," said Dick.

I helped him secure the motor to the transom of his canoe. Dick's vintage gas paddle lacked the convenience of a neutral gear, which meant he had to be offshore to start it. As I pushed him out into the waves he said, "You better stay here until I'm underway, I might need rescuing."

"Dick, can you swim?" I called loudly.

"Not very well," replied Dick.

Yikes, all I could think of was the feeble attempt I could make at a rough-water rescue with a one-person kayak and my "fisherman grade" life vest.

What came next was not a comforting scene. Dick was thirty feet offshore yanking on the pull starter while the canoe was bouncing in the waves and spinning out of control. It was at least five minutes before he got the motor to fire. When it did the canoe began buzzing in circles! With Dick in the rear and no counterweight in the front, the canoe would leap high out of the water before banging downward into the next big wave. What a sight!

I watched as he slowly crept forward to the center of the canoe where he was able to grab hold of two steering lines that he had attached to the motor. With Dick finally in his navigating position he could turn the bow into the wind and regain control of the canoe. I breathed a sigh of relief, but I stayed and watched his tiny canoe make its way up the center of the lake, disappearing and reappearing as it climbed up and over the tops of large rolling waves.

As I reflected on it that evening, I came to realize that what had seemed like a terrifying experience to me was just another afternoon on the lake for Dick. Upper Twin Lake was doing what it usually does at this time of day and so was Dick, making a routine canoe ride up or down the lake, just has he had done time and again for three decades. I was watching *one man in his wilderness.*

[Authors Note: The two lines that Dick attached to his outboard were actually to control the throttle. Dick ran the lines through a pulley he attached to the motor housing which allowed him to advance or retract the throttle level from mid-ship by pulling on either the right or left line respectively. Dick steered the canoe with a four-foot wooden pole that he slipped over the motor's tiller handle.]

* * *

Many radio calls, hikes, and canoe paddles with Dick would follow in the coming months that summer. He took me on my first trip to the head of the Upper Lake and showed me the cove where many years earlier a Hawaiian couple had died from exposure. He said they were the only people he knew of that had died at Twin Lakes.

I was with him when a group of people visiting from Georgia gave him several huge bags of processed food—the sort of food that normally doesn't make its way to Twin Lakes. Dick acted like a little kid at Christmas, digging items out of the bags one at a time. He asked me more than once what some of the things were, like blue corn tortilla chips or penne pasta. His most frequent line was "Let's try it." We split everything up or bantered for those that were one-of-a-kind.

Another time Dick fried up a Dolly Varden for us while I contributed some lentil pilaf leftovers. The fish was delicious! Dick's seasonings were superb! (Salt, pepper, chili powder and some flour) He liked the pilaf—with ketchup—and I left the rest with him.

One day just after I arrived, a small black bear paid a visit to Dick's while he was away from the cabin. It knocked a box off one of his outside tables. The bear wasn't afraid of Dick, and he said he chased it around the cabin three times. A couple of campers helped shout it away, and the bear ran off into the bushes. I went with Dick to the camp site near Hope Creek and we found the bear there amidst some unsettled campers.

I will never forget the day he took me and friend on a guided tour of Low Pass, one of his favorite hikes. Dick was out ahead of us, but he stopped abruptly. When we reached him he was pointing at a small rock pinnacle that stuck out from the side of a mountain to the east. "See that man up there, it's the Sentinel that guards the pass, we need to give the password before we can go any farther." Dick was in good humor that day, and after I gave him a big hug he said the password was "Swordfish." We stopped there and had some lunch while sitting in the sun.

We made it into the pass, but on the way out it seemed like Dick was slipping and tripping all over. I kept an eye on him, but he insisted on bringing up the rear. At one point while crossing a steep scree slope with loose rocks I heard a noise. I turned around to see Dick lying on the ground several feet below the trail. I called back, "Dick, what happened, do you need help? "No," he replied, "I was trying to slide down the mountain but something stopped me." He was so funny!

* * *

September came much sooner than I had wanted, and along with it came the end of my season at Twin Lakes. I left by ten in the morning for what would be my final boat trip to the Upper Lake and Dick's. He had called me before I left on his radio to say that he had caught a lake trout and was keeping it to teach me his filleting technique.

Dick greeted me at the beach with a hug. It was apparent that he realized this was our last meeting. We chatted and ate lunch, then we went looking for the mysterious "voices" I said I thought I had heard. Something sounded to me like men talking. We hiked the loop to Spike's cabin and back. Mystery solved; it was a love-sick moose. Dick certainly enjoyed this at my expense.

The wind was calm, so we launched the boat and took a tour up to the head of the lake. Dick sat in front of me on the floor of the boat and admired the scenery going by. He occasionally pointed to a mountain slope or a point along the shoreline and spoke of moose, bears, wolves, and hikes of the past. At the head of the lake we got out on the beach and looked around. He found an old platform that he said was there when he first moved to Twin Lakes. It was deteriorating then and only a small portion of it was still standing.

He led me over to check out the old beaver lodge for new activity. There was no new wood added, but some freshly stripped alder twigs announced that one was around. As we pulled up, a bald eagle landed on a tree but soon flew off. It had been feeding on dead salmon. In the shallows along the lake shore, we counted eighteen sockeye (red) salmon. Most were showing signs of their long journey from the sea and battles for spawning sites. They were nearing death. A Red-Necked Grebe was swimming near the salmon. Dick said it would stay until freeze-up.

On the way back down the lake Dick suggested that we stop at a set of cabins (Wind Song Lodge, owned by Gary Titus) near the mouth of Falls Creek. Dick looked around there and found the boat that we had searched for at the head of the lake back in July. Dick grabbed the keys to the cabins and I followed along as he checked things over, looking for water leaks, mouse problems, or porcupine damage.

As we walked back to the boat Dick picked up some bullet casings left behind by the last occupants. Before climbing into the boat we sat on a bench swing near the beach. It afforded a panoramic view of Hope Creek Valley and Crag Mountain, Dick's "home" on the south shore of the Upper Lake. Dick said he could stay till the end of time swinging on that bench.

The sun was dropping below the mountain as I motored across the lake to drop Dick off on his beach. He didn't want me to go. It was very sad to say goodbye there. Tears came to my eyes. As I pulled out I said, "*Au Revoir Mon Ami*" (Goodbye my friend.) I realized that I might never see him standing on the shore again, waving good-bye.

Jana Walker was a seasonal Park Ranger stationed at Lower Twin Lake during Dick's final extended summer stay at his cabin. Jana's daily journal reveals the close bond that developed between them. Her frequent visits to his cabin and their morning radio chats enriched Dick's final months at Twin Lakes, a time in his life when he may not have preferred to be alone in the wilderness.

Epilogue

September 25. Clear, calm and 45 degrees. Just finished the break-fast dishes when I heard the plane. Time to go. I put the covers over the windows, secured the stove pipe, and carried in a fresh supply of wood. A last check on the woodshed. The weasel whisked into the woodpile, switched ends, and peered out at me. I could hear the squirrel singing from a cluster of spruce cones. At last he was rid of me. I closed my door and turned the locking lever for the last time. RLP

One morning a few years ago a floatplane pulled up onto the beach in front of Dick's cabin. The first person to climb out onto the floats was Lori, an eleven-year-old girl from the East Coast. Dick Proenneke was her hero. Lori had watched his films over and over, and read and re-read his book cover to cover. She had pictures of Dick and his cabin on the walls of her bedroom and she even had a Dick Proenneke T-shirt.

At the time we were serving as docents at the Proenneke Site. We gave Lori and her parents a brief tour of the cabin, but we never asked Lori what it was about Dick that drew her so close to him. Perhaps it was his love for the wild animals that he lived with in his Twin Lakes wilderness. It might have been his stunning photographs or the animated tales of some of his favorite animals. Such as the day he wrote in his journal *"of all the birds and animals at Twin Lakes I would like to be a young owl in a nest protected from a down lake wind."*

Lori explicitly remembered little Milo the weasel with whom Dick played cat and mouse. She also recalled the tug-of-war he engaged in with a wolverine in the middle of the night after it grabbed a piece of meat he had tied to the end of a line extending under the cabin door. It's likely she was touched by how Dick treated young Leon and Sig Alsworth when they came to stay with him one summer. She may have even fantasized about being along with them when they picked blueberries or paddled up the lake.

Lori's parents told us that they put a little card under the Christmas tree the year that she turned eleven. When she opened it on Christmas Eve she was momentarily speechless. It read: "You're going to see Dick's cabin next summer, love mom and dad." The months leading up to their trip to Alaska passed slowly. Lori prepared meticulously. She closely looked at photographs of the interior of Dick's cabin and even made a list of his tools and personal belongings that she wanted to see.

They arrived in Anchorage in early August and flew out to a fishing lodge near Lake Iliamna where they would spend a week. One day was set aside for a trip to Twin Lakes, and Lori reminded their pilot/guide of that promptly at the start of every day. When Lori's long awaited day-trip to Twin Lakes finally arrived, their pilot said he had some bad news. As often happens in late summer on the Alaska Peninsula, the weather had turned sour. At breakfast all the lodge guests were told that because of high winds, rain, and low visibility, no planes would be flying. The next morning the weather was even worse.

Not unlike the weather, it's next to impossible to change vacation schedules, commercial airline tickets, and lodge reservations. On their Saturday departure date their pilot had to fly them back to Anchorage and return with a new group of guests. Lori was in tears as she handed her backpack to the pilot. He finished loading the Dehavilland Beaver and walked over to speak with the other guests that would be on the flight to Anchorage.

He walked back to Lori and her parents and said, "We can divert up to Twin Lakes and stop at Dick's cabin on the way back to Anchorage." But he added, "We can only stay for few minutes."

Lorie's tears turned to jubilance. If Dick had been standing on his beach when they landed that day she would have jumped into his arms and given him a big hug. Next she would have asked Dick if he would take her into his cabin, show her the saw he used to rip boards, his door latch, snow shovel, and ladders. Had time allowed, she might have asked him to take her to Teetering Rock or for a paddle up the lake.

It has been many years since Dick last greeted visitors on his beach or sat at his desk, pen in hand, making notes on the weather or the family of brown bears he saw on a morning hike up Hope Creek Valley. Today a National Park Service ranger or volunteer might greet you. But when you arrive at his beach, whether it be by air, boat, or on foot, your senses might be fooled into thinking Dick never left.

His overturned canoe is there; that used to be a sign that maybe he was nearby. You walk up to the front of the cabin and stop to admire his pair of spruce burl tables. The cabin door is unlocked, so you enter and walk over to his desk. A guest book is open and alongside it a map with a stickpin labeled "Here Today." You're momentarily distracted by that view down lake from his desk chair. As you turn around you see his plaid wool shirt hanging from a wooden peg on the wall and his sleeping bag unrolled on the top bunk. You touch his wood stove, it's cold but it looks like he might have used it that morning. It appears as though Dick might be out on a hike.

Dick's log work, stone chimney, ladders, wooden spoons, desk chair, hand-crimped pans, and even the gravel on the floor of his cabin all silently speak to those who know the intimate details of his life. Hundreds travel to see Dick's Twin Lakes wilderness each year. For some his cabin is the destination, for others it's a starting point. For young or old it's often the trip of a lifetime.

Dick's cabin and the land immediately surrounding it were listed on the National Register of Historic Places in 2007. National Historic Sites are places recognized by the National Park Service for their significance in American History. The listing was in recognition of the craftsmanship of Dick's cabin and his voice in the preservation of wilderness in Alaska.

A copy of the book *A Sand County Almanac* rests on Dick's bookshelf. Its author, conservationist and wilderness advocate Aldo Leopold once wrote: "*The greatest challenge to mankind is to live on a piece of land without spoiling it.*" Dick achieved not only that in his thirty years at Twin Lakes; his cabin and the life he led there have become a symbol of wilderness in Lake Clark National Park and Preserve.

Dicks Letters

We often wonder how many letters Dick wrote during his years at Twin Lakes. If it were possible to gather them all up and place them on a scale, it's likely their weight would exceed that of his journals. Dick's letters were interesting, detailed, and beautiful. Sky blue ink from his Sheaffer Triumph fountain pen flowed across the pages like ripples on a lake. A header on the upper right side of the letter usually read "Twin Lakes" or "The Log House" along with the date and weather conditions. They were usually signed *Dick P.* Even for those who struggled to decipher his handwriting, Dick letters had an artistic quality.

Dick's letters kept friends and family closely connected to his life and the seasonal cycle of natural events at Twin Lakes. No tribute to Dick would be complete without a sampling of his letters and acknowledging how they enriched the lives of those who knew him. Like his journals, Dick's letters are a window into the past. But unlike his journals, they have a more open and candid quality. Some of Dick's longest running correspondents were his friends from Kodiak Island Norma and Jerry Holt and Spike and Hope Carrithers. The names of many of the contributors to this book are woven into the text of these letters and on more than one occasion they are linked to a humorous tale.

Twin Lakes   May 18, 1985

Dear Norma & Jerry;

   Snowing this morning and 32°. Now at ten it has faired a bit
and may be a nice afternoon. It snowed all day yesterday (3")
accompanied by a strong wind from the gulf and I wondered about
the new lambs and probably caribou calves not yet strong enough
to stand.

   Thank you for your nice Christmas card of Dec. 8th while
you were in Anchorage hoping for space available to Japan. Around
three in the afternoon several big jets cross here headed in that
direction – perhaps you could have seen Twin Lakes if you were
properly oriented. Hope you had a nice trip and arrived back safely
about May 1st as planned.

   Here at the lakes it was an unusual winter and still is from
the appearance this morning. Snow came after that big storm late
last summer. One inch at lake level and drifts from it stayed at the
1600 foot level.

   After an early cool spell it turned mild and freeze up of this
lake came Dec. 14th after the lower lake closed up during a very
brief cold spell in early Nov. Fifty six inches of snow in Dec. and
naturally several inches would come on thin ice to load it and the
snow become saturated. My mail and Christmas grub supply came
by copter. Wayne Alsworth (Babe's eldest son) learned to drive and
traded a beautiful Beech Bonanza for an early model Bell. Dec. 23rd
and a white out with strong wind. Imagine my surprise to hear a
plane engine close and then see the flashing beacon appear out of
the gloom. Glen and Bee (Wayne) trying out that rig in fixed wing
non flying weather. Glen reported no problem. My Xmas turkey
was a spruce grouse rooster that had a mid-air with my clothes line
and broke his neck. Stuffed solid with spruce needles so you can
imagine the flavor.

   January was tropical. Morning ave. of better than +29° for
the month. To make matters worse it rained considerable on the
deep snow and the sheep would work over time making a living for
the rest of the winter.

Feb. was the winter one with -44° and a morning ave. temp. of -30° for nearly three weeks. March came in mild but ended averaging about zero degrees. More snow and the ice slowly building. The snow fall for the snow season is well over 170 inches now – perhaps June will see the final addition. Snow pack 53 inches at best but for the most part 46 to 48 inches.

May started quite cool and no small migrating birds arrived until the 13th. A robin was first and a golden crowned sparrow second followed by white-crowned sparrows and Oregon Juncos. The first waterfowl I saw on the lakes were a white fronted goose and a Common goldeneye drake followed soon after by pintails, buffleheads, mallards, shovelers and more.

True to form the first lamb on the mountain came May 10th and last year the same. Then a few days before the next and last year the same. So, one old girl must be early. Till now five lambs or at least until yesterday and the snow storm.

A caribou herd came to the lower lake and how many is a good question. Many on both sides and caribou continually crossing the lake ice. A few years ago Will Troyer, Park Service biologist and I went to Turquoise Lake (next north) on May 15th to see the herd calving. Calves the 15th but during the following week hundreds and hundreds of new calves. But here as of two days ago I saw not one new calf and I had a perfect opportunity to see them. A bear was hunting calves and as he loped and circled in land the caribou poured out on the ice. He found no calves that I was aware of and I saw none with the hundreds that moved out on the lake. That bear knows that if he stays with the herd he will find many new calves. He showed not the slightest interest in the mature and yearling caribou ahead of him. He knew what he was looking for.

Bears came out late this time. From mid-April on I was on watch for sign of spring bear. Last Oct. I had followed the tracks of five that had gone up the far shore. Tracks made over a period of a week or more. Three sets of tracks were those of a sow and six month and more old cubs. Up the lake and the right fork of the river *about six miles above the lake. Not until the last week have I seen sign but one track was old and probably the bear came out early in May.*

While searching for new lambs from the lake on May 15th I spotted a big brown sow and new twins on the mt. across and down. The cubs looked larger than April cubs I have seen in the past. Both black as black bear cubs but with that white collar that reminds me of the Hampshire hog. Very active little guys and already when I saw them, they knew that snow was made for cubs to play in. I saw a cub fight, their dog fight voices and them tumbling down the slope tied in a knot. Next day I spotted the den no more than a short quarter mile from the Bears. A south facing slope as all dens seem to be located and about 1000 ft. above the lake.

That one I must examine. I know of no less than ten sites on the mountain across the lake where bears have denned in the past. Yesterday morning before the blizzard I saw the big brown (dark blond) sow snuggled up against the base of a big rock face but she has moved and I hope to relocate her today. So it goes at Twin Lakes – always the same but always different and interesting.

Closing for now and wishing you folks good health and a good summer on Kodiak

My best,

Dick P.

* * *

Twin Lakes   *Feb. 19, 1986*

Dear Norma & Jerry-

It is high time I was writing to you. Seems I never get caught up on letters. Always another batch coming in and among them some that demand a prompt reply. Plane day is due and past so I am gaining on the back log. Thank you for writing and your river otter card. I see one here now and again. Just last summer one was rolling and diving at the mouth of Hope Creek. They are nothing but smooth action in water. I have a few Martin here too, but have only seen one till now.

Kodiak must have had a very wet year to break all records. Strange how one can forget when a bright day shows Kodiak at its best. I see in "Senior Voice" paper that your Seniors say Kodiak is the ideal place to retire. I never thought of it as such when I was wallowing in the rain and mud working on breakdowns, but to own a sturdy boat and go where the wind goes is something else. That Kodiak I would like any time.

Here, winter came very early as it did in the south 48. Late Oct. and early Nov. was real winter with -23° These lakes closed up weeks earlier than ever before. Then moderating temps and unsafe ice and snow on ice and saturation which is always bad news. Then came Dec. with a 27.22° morning ave. temp. and Jan. with a 12° ave Wind most continuous and sheep country snow free. Never have I seen less snow on the big pasture across. Here at lake level the snow pack 23" at present and the lake ice 20 inches. Feb. got off with a 28.9° morning ave. for 10 days but now clear calm and cooler to -12° this morning.

I have had a supply problem this winter. No snow at Port Alsworth and for a long, long time no ice worth using in Babe's bay for skis. So it was wheels on every thing. The Park Service cub had retractable skis so it was Hollis (Twitchell) of the Park Service who came. I had as much as 18" of snow on the ice here. They had left me a Motorola Walkie Talkie to keep them off of thin ice and it came in handy just after freeze up Nov. 3. I knew a patch of 5 inch ice that filled the little bite beyond Hope Creek. Hollis came and reported it looking pretty spooky down there, open water and two and three inch ice else where. So I promised him a new cub if he delivered my mail. The first in a month.

All for now and wishing you good health and ideal Kodiak weather. Best of health and good luck to the boys and Darcy too.

Sincerely,

Dick P.

* * *

Twin Lakes   *July 2, 1986*

Dear Norma & Jerry –

Guess it was last mail call that a letter came from Spike & Hope. She mentioned you have a plane now so how about launching over this way some time. Wish I could say there will be scads of blue berries but if so there will have to be many more berries than blossoms but some years it seems that there are.

Sure did enjoy your trip to the Orient. I wonder about the Philippines and will our lease be renewed for bases there. If not it seems the Ruskies will get them in due course of time. Our Lake Clark Natl. Park Superintendent and wife have a daughter going to school in Bangkok this year. Paul (Haertel) and Margot, his wife, are home stead sitting ex Gov. Jay Hammond's place on Miller Creek (Lake Clark) again this summer when Jay, Bella, Heidi and husband Bruce fish at Naknek.

Here, it has been a real nice summer till now. It's the dry season of course and usually there is lots of snow to go so little rain is needed. This time though there wasn't all that much snow. About 100 inch total snow fall with 31" the snow pack at best. Last year had 160" or better. 39 ½ inches of ice and it was gone by June 12th. A fair lamb crop of about 18 on the MTS. across and I hear from the park service that many sheep (more than 100) attended the big rendezvous at the lick over Turquoise way. I trekked over June 20th but saw only 45 that day. Which was about a week later than they (P. S.) were looking down. Two very near full curl rams were there when I visited. Molting, mud to the knees and eyes, they were anything but the great rams I see in Nov.

The green of summer is at its best. Wild roses are just starting to bloom. Not many visitors yet but July and August is the season. A few have written of coming. Betsy of Austin Texans July 14th to camp at the lower end of this lake. A few more threatening to come but I don't get excited about that kind. Bob Acheson's daughter Jill Acheson Berkin has written that she is coming from

Kodiak to use their cabin (Spikes) September 5 to 12*th*. That is late and storms are common but it is also Fall Color time and can be beautiful if the weather cooperates.

Fishing has been good till now. Lake Trout are active from breakup till too warm weather. The best run of salmon I have ever seen here last year and now clouds of little dark minnows must be the hatch from last summers run.

The caribou herd moved by the lower end about June 21*st* and headed northwest. Leon Alsworth was flying sight seers from Houston and reported thousands of cows and calves. 37,000 was the total as of last years count.

I'll call this good for now. Do hope it finds you folks well and studying the charts that cover Lake Clark country. Its been a long time. So, see you later, I hope.

Best to you,

Dick

* * *

Twin Lakes   3/31/87

Dear Norma & Jerry

No less than 4 Holt letters looking at me and I guess you know I'm uncomfortable. Last spring and nearly a year ago I was going to even the score and then a letter came saying you were on your way west on a big adventure. So, I would wait until you returned which you have and quite some time ago. So, lets get with it even though the sky is clear, the sun very white on a new dusting of snow and the temp. this morning 15°. Its a day to travel and I must this afternoon. Till now since Christmas my pedometer reads 847 miles.

I read your Christmas form letter with great interest. Norma, you just must write a best seller of your adventures. Just last mail had a royalty check and a note, "From Tokyo Publisher" Royalty is 33 ⅓% instead of 5% which is some different.

Of your trip the one thing that really caught my eye was, "The penalty for smuggling drugs is death" Now, that is making it plain enough and I wonder why more countries don't follow their lead.??? And the action at Clark Air Force Base "people power in action," read real good and I would agree with that. I'm wondering if some time in the not too distant future that the Russians will be occupying our bases there??

So now you are in business on Kodiak and I hope it goes well for you. Just this last Alaska Mag. had a story "Kodiak Island Services" And, I was surprised at what is going on there in the line of new business as compared to 1966 when I was working there last. I noticed that the Author Jim Reardon didn't mention the good weather erasing the bad which it did each and every time.

I wonder who bought Spike and Hope's old home on Saw Mill Lake and if it looks pretty much like it did when they lived there. It was a nice location.

Little airplanes are built to <u>fail!</u> When I bent up my J-3 and later saw it stripped of fabric I thought it should have been built more like a Cat than a kite. Hope you have your plane flying by now and that summer will see you land at Twin Lakes some fine day.

1986 was a good fall color year with weather much better than common for Mid Sept. Many light frosts in late Aug. and early Sept. – then very mild until Nov. when the lower lake iced over Nov. 20th. Mild again with most constant wind from the gulf. This lake closed up Christmas day. I had seven moose here on the point that day. One a fine bull and gentle which big bulls seldom are.

A large wolverine came to visit one night. Crunching snow crust told me company was coming. At 8 feet he stood looking into the light and not a bit spooky.

Three wolves killed a cow moose in mid Feb. One wolf making tracks 6 X 5 ¼". A year ago I made a cast of tracks that size and three wolves then also. Those are my dogs, I think.

March and 10 days of clear, calm and -22° ave. (morning) The low -29° That was the only typical winter weather. Lake ice as of now 28" and snow pack 20". Ice will be out about mid June I suspect.

Norma, your good cookies have gone the way of all good cookies and the high bush too. I'm returning your cookie box and empty container. With them a sample of Twin Lakes blue berry jam. Some one sent me some jam made from domestically grown blue berries from Rhode Island. Alaskan berries have more flavor, and a lot more.

That's about it I guess. Do hope this finds you folks and your boys & girls doing great. Good health first and foremost.

Sincerely,

Dick P.

* * *

Twin lakes   June 30, 1990

Dear Spike and Hope-

It is 3 PM and the temp. a rare 76 – that's warm! Yesterday was about the same. A breeze down and cotton clouds all about. I climbed high on Bell mt. to inspect last winter's quarters for the mother and coming two year-old twins. What a place to sleep 6 months. Bears are like people when it comes to living quarters Best part of the climb was finding some loaded blueberry bushes on the way down.

Thank you for the good letter and birthday card. Evidently it has been a while since a letter went your way for I see no "check" [an actual check mark in the letter] indicating answered. Hope, your eye must be back to battery by now. Surgery on eyes does not come cheap either and just imagine the guy doing a half dozen before lunch. It would be interesting to learn what the record is for making money in a short length of time. Last letter from Robert had his eye pressure 25 which is getting right up there and time to watch it. Dorothy was doing fine. Duplicate bills still coming in and each marked "This is not a bill. Insurance had paid it. At time of writing, the total was more than $63,000.^{00} averaging more than $2,000.^{00} per day in the hospital. Bills or duplicates from doctors they never heard of. What prevents a doctor from inviting a friend to submit a bill for what ever reason?

Not one lamb at the sheep rendezvous at the lick in mid June. Only three ewes eating the weak calcium mud. Lots of caribou calves and also grizzly bears mingling with the herd, some with cubs. I saw a moose calf track on my beach and also on the gravel bar near Frank Bell's old tumble down cabin on the Chilly River. The calf here made tracks in my garden and sampled the sugar snap pea's. I certainly had a good crop of red radishes which are about gone. My three hills of spuds are up and being fed Glens good "Conklin" liquid fertilizer "FEAST." It certainly produced a crop for him last summer.

Glen has acquired another twin engine Piper and that makes 4 twins plus the Otter 9 passenger, a couple Cessna 206's (4 passenger) Babe's old 180, a piper two seater on floats and another little T craft, similar to Babe's little black bird and I assume he got it special for Babe to fly when he and Mary come this fishing and berry season. I hear they are going to stay longer this time. Glen has 8 pilots flying for him. They take care of the rotation of sport fishermen for several lodges. Now if they can just go the season without wrecking one or more. I did have the runway looking real good to start the season and I have heard since it is good still. Will the grader man get credit for helping making it the best season ever? Doubt it very much – not religious enough.

Here the tourist season is starting. A big Cessna came to Titus Point and I see the cover is away from the door opening. "Alaska West Airs" big Otter has hauled several loads of material for the most expensive shop (Gary insists it will be a shop and not a *bunkhouse for Clients.) I can hardly see Gary and Christina getting off work at this very busy tourist time on the Kenai so maybe it is friends of theirs who came for the 4th of July.*

Terry Lichana producer of the TV show "Austin City Limits" should be at the mouth of Emerson with two of his crew. A letter from him had Glen flying him in yesterday evening and a plane did come late.

A couple were here for a few hrs from Kennewick, Wash. The woman a Mexican Civil Engineer and said she would send me some Wash. apples.

A couple from Calif too and came up with Patricia Brown the Twin Lakes ranger for the season. A couple from Fairbanks wanting to fly down for the day and an Ed Burns from North Carolina who with his wife will be visiting their son in Fair banks.

Fishing was real good just after the ice went out and the lake was rising. It is off now but I haven't worked at it as I would if I was real hungry.

I volunteered to clean up Frank bell's tumbled down cabin on the Chilly below the lower lake. The job has been completed except for someone burning the pile of no good wood and air lifting by helicopter the sound logs to the ranger cabin which is short of fire wood. They may think it too expensive, burn it and buy oil.

Chin-up's a batch. I worked at it regular doing 50, then comes the real test and you will read about it in Journal 91. [Editor's note: Dicks 75th birthday meaning he would have to do 75 chin-ups.]

The lake is sparkling from a white capping breeze now at 4:15 temp. 74°. Wishing you folks the best and a real good summer and fall season.

Here, about the same
        Dick

* * *

Twin Lakes   *August 17, 1990*

Dear Spike and Hope-

And the lake is right up into the brush. Wouldn't it be a disaster if it didn't back down to winter low? It has been full for a couple of days now and no rain. But it was a 12 hr. rain that made it full and quickly. I have never seen the lake come up so fast. It must have been a down pour in the high ones Hope Creek washed my skinny bridge out and now the stream bed is to wide for the pole. Have to get the Engineering Dept. working.

Two letters from you since I last wrote. Activities put my letter writing on hold for a spell. Esther was here from Aug. 10ᵗʰ to 20ᵗʰ and since there has been visiting hikers and kayakers. Two, Jim and Jack from Oakland Ca., are up Hope Creek now after me taking them up the hump to show them the teetering one and split rock. They decided to go on up the left side. If they get to the glaciers they will be late coming down. Patricia works at it sending visitors up my way to sign my guest book. Just a few days ago a Chinese Dr. and son, from Mayo Clinic were here. A good man with a camera that doctor. A Dermatologist is his profession. He says the sun is the big trouble maker. That heavy tan is not good for you. Would you believe that he has been in every National. Park in the U.S.A.?

[Inserted apparently by Hope] This was the night I called 911. Sure thought I'd lost him.

Spike I can imagine you waking up to see lots of visitors by your bed side. At 4 AM that would be a surprise. Like you I think that would be a very comfortable way to go. Put me on the waiting list. Never heard of "Apnea" or of those symptoms. One must be in a very relaxed state while it is doing its bit. Like me in Providence after I bent the J-3 severely. They had me in the whirl pool bath and it. too warm. The attendant lady was in another room helping another attendant and left me quite awhile. I knew it was hot but I figured nows the chance to cook my beginning of arthritis they had predicted for me later. I was red as a beet when they found me and rolled off of the wagon into my bed like so much Jello. Relaxed.

Never did get arthritis or any trace of it.

Hope, sounds like you got a good fix on your eye. That job done with out help to pay would be a batch. A man here from Minn. just had the same surgery. 20 min worth for I think he said $2,700.00 but the doctor gave him a sample of the lens put in to show friends and prospective customers. He told me how many the doctor did in a half day. He must have some one working full time counting his income. Katie Pante in Oregon (Prineville) [Inserted apparently by Hope] had the same as you and reports that it was a great success. Now for the other one.

* * *

Twin Lakes   *March 15, 1991, 2 PM -6°*

Dear Spike and Hope.

Beautiful day after a very stormy night. 19° when I climbed the ladder and a -23° at revile. That's a lot of cold suddenly. A gale force wind ushered it in.

Glen is due in to pick up Patty, the ranger, tomorrow or Sunday. He flew her in the 9th. She snowshoed up the 11th and yes, she brought some thing's for the cooking pot and also her sleeping bag.

Too nippy to put her in Spikes cabin, so I gave her my bunk and I got a cot from Spikes cabin. She was here two nights and it snowed an extra 4 inches the last night so I packed her gear while she broke trail towards the ranger cabin. I went half way and she took it from there. It sounded as if she and Evan will get married, but where? She would prefer it to be here at Twin Lakes.

Gary (Titus) is over at his homestead and has been for nearly two months. Gong home to Sterling last of March. By then he will have that new lower cabin (back and inland maybe 100 feet from where Jerre Wills had his cabin and slightly higher above lake level.) Christina and her twin sister Lorrie were over for a week and

left late in Feb. A good pair those two, not identical twins but close.
Lorrie is a veterinarian and birds are her favorite. Has worked a lot
with swan poisoned by lead shot.

Would you believe we had readings as high as 50° in Feb.
(after the 20th) Snow pack now is 34" in the wood's and snow fall
about 125" till now Lake ice about 35". I am still getting water from
the lake at the mouth of Hope Creek. The snow is deep there and
the water hole stays open if I shovel some snow in after each use.

The State is interested in an airport at Port Alsworth. They
would buy "Bee's" strip and additional land to make it 155 acres.
Bee will be a rich man again. His recent venture was a big
helicopter which he bought in Texas and also a truck to haul it for it
was not assembled. His and Bettie's daughter Mary Lorene got
married recently. A second marriage for him. – has a couple of
children and a drinking problem so she will no doubt think of those
who advised, _don't do it!_

Wild ones are very scarce this winter. No moose up this far,
but Gary and I saw 15 along the north side of the lower lake.
Rabbits have never come back up to peak population which is true
on the Kenai, Also.

So, no lynx cats and foxes are scare. Wolverines are still
here. They cleaned up a ¾ curl ram across that I think go caught by
an avalanche.

I have been thinking Spike & Hope have an anniversary
about now and checked my address book to find it March 31st and
the 62nd. That's nice I must say _congratulations_ and may they
continue on & on. Lots of letters to write but none more important
than this one to let you know I didn't for get.

So, closing for now and wishing you two the best of
everything good. Hope you have a good and early spring season.

My very best,

Dick

P.S. Someone said Spike* passed the driving test – glad to hear of it may you use this last ticket to the end and no fender benders.

*[Inserted by Hope] Yes he did & can still drive

* * *

Twin Lakes   Dec 12, 1991, 7:20 PM, clear, 12°

Dear Spike & Hope-

Seldom write letters after supper but better do it. Some letters from last Christmas have not been answered! More than one hour till "taps" and what better way to spend it than writing you two a short one at least.

Snowing these days. About a foot since the 1st of Dec. 8 inches in the past 3 days. Till now no rain on snow but it will come soon enough.

It was Leon who delivered my mail Dec. 1st and your package. A heavy little rascal and it is in quarantine. Spikes cabin is good storage before the grand opening. One came from my Sis. Florence and I unwrapped it till I got to green Xmas. paper and stopped. Esther Caparelli sent a heavy one and my guess is some straw berry jam in glass and I keep telling her, "don't do it!" Seems heavy for cookies. From Sequin Wash. and Harold Davis (ex Alaskan) dried apples of his own drying for sure. Said he was going to do it. Be sure to put a price on them I wrote. The mission girls have threatened to do some baking and candy making and how is my supply?

What will the winter be? A -23° the low till now. Last year a -45° the last day of November.

If "Freddy" (my resident squirrel) knows anything about it this will be an easy winter. Last two fall seasons saw a heap of spruce cones come to his cache near the wood shed. This time very few if any. He brought a lot of last winter's cones on top from under ground and there they were in a heap when the snows started. Other squirrels were doing the same.

Moose have moved down country I guess for I see very little sign up this far. Leon and Alan Bennett the biologist are due to fly moose survey down the Chilly soon.

It's so white on the south slope across I don't look for sheep. Probably they are on the big pasture.

Again this year a poor showing of snow shoe hare tracks on this side. I have seen very few fox tracks and no lynx tracks. Snow shoes started to build their population but something went wrong I guess.

Gary and Christina are going to Seattle for Xmas. Laurie (Christinas twin sister) will be there too. Their father lives there after living a long time in northern Minnesota.

Hope – now you have two new eyes, right? Hope this last one was a great success. Robt. was going to get an implant in his good eye.

I'll close with a special wish for your health, a real agreeable holiday season and may spring come early.

Till later - Dick   --//--

Merry Christmas

* * *

Twin Lakes   Nov. 5, 1992

Dear Hope-

Thank you a batch for your good last letter which fell from above. Leon and Clair did the honors and will again soon. I have a batch of out going that must go down to the ranger cabin for pickup.

This lake is still open but the lower lake was completely frozen over as of yesterday. The weather turned tropical and one 5-acre pool stayed open for a few days. I was down yesterday to check the older ice and found it 2 to 3 inches. Not enough for the Park Service cub. They want it 4 ½ to 5 inches. Much less chance of having to write lots of letters asking "how come you did what you did?" The Park Service is holding several packages and I must tell them to make touch and goes, don't stop, drop the packages the three feet to the ice as I will go get them. Hollis used to do that and it worked perfect. A plane on skis can land on 2 inches of ice and won't break through until it stops, soo , don't Stop!

Thanks for cashing the ten dollar check. I too have problem's with checking back to get my check record some what straight. I have sent signed checks, on occasion, and let the receiver fill in the amount. That was good, I knew the person or thought I did. Then, one guy raised the agreed on price $10.^{00} Not too expensive lesson but here after I will be more spooky.

Have you heard from Raymond recently? After flying "Mark Air" from Anchorage to LA for $120.^{05} he had his Toyota pick up stolen nearly the first time he used it. Parked at a market parking lot and locked it. Didn't get back for about 30 min and it was gone. "Lucky" the name of the market. The police said they would probably find it in a few days. They did and in an alley about a mile and one half from 3569 Norton. It had been stripped of nearly all usable parts. He sold the shell for $100.00. Bet you the guy who bought it knew where he could find the missing parts. Twin Lakes was never like that. He did get a good price for the antique J-3 cub $24,^{000} with wheels and floats. Floats worth $5,000.^{00}.

I think a person is as old as they feel. I certainly don't feel that I am coming 77 next May. I carry on doing the same work and play that I have for 20 yrs and see little difference. – except it takes a little longer to bounce back after going with out sleep for too long. No aches or pains as a regular thing but some times over do a bit in packing in wood etc. Then it comes about not by the packing but getting to my feet with a heavy pack on my back. I used some of Spike's 454 and I reckon it helped. I have some thing similar sent to me by Robert whose neighbor gave it to him. "Mineral Ice" is the name. – a pretty blue color and cool. Remember "Sloan's liniment" hot! and you could smell it from way out.

Raymond put his sourdough starter in the frig. when he left Lynwood in later part of June. Got back to it Sept. 26th and mixed it up. It came back in a few days. So, if it is kept cool enough so as not to mold it will stay alive for a good long spell.

It was a pretty crazy fall season. Fall colors never did amount to much. Froze too hard early Colors were snow covered when they should have been good. Green leaves froze solid and stayed green zero degrees the morning of Sept. 26th and a morning ave. of 8° for the week. Not since have I had a week with such low readings, +6°, +5°, +7° & 0°. The geese and swan didn't come and pond's and small lakes were icing so strong that float planes wouldn't land. The state let helicopters pick up stranded hunters. Then came Oct. and mild. The Swan and geese came on schedule. Lots of them and was it that many young ones that were yet in shape for the flight. I think it is a pretty close schedule getting to the nesting grounds and away to beat the ice.

So, the bears are in and I don't know of a den across the lake. Snow layer about 8-9 inches in the woods. In less than a week no more sun till Feb. 93.

End is near I see, so Best of every thing good to you. Have a real good rest of fall. Walk a lot for exercise is good for a body.

My best wishes,
    Dick

-----//-----

P.P.S. I heard Frank Bell was past 90 yrs. Too old to go when he did. He knew, I think.

About the Editors

Alan Bennett spent thirteen years working for Lake Clark National Park and Preserve as a wildlife biologist, fisheries biologist, and program manager for inventory and monitoring. During his tenure he wrote the Parks first Natural Resources Management Plan, designed and completed a resource inventory of its marine coastline, and wrote its long-term Vital Signs Monitoring Plan. After retiring he spent a portion of the next six summers as a volunteer interpretive guide at the Richard Proenneke Site. When he was not giving visitors a tour, he repeated photographs taken by Dick in the 1960's and 1970's to document how a warming climate has transformed the Twin Lakes landscape that Dick experienced into what visitors see today.

Laurel Bennett spent 10 years working for Lake Clark National Park & Preserve as a biological technician, part time cultural resources technician and an aquatic ecologist for the inventory and monitoring program. She wrote the first Cultural Resources Management Plan for the Park and initiated the aquatic monitoring program. She joined Alan for a portion of six summers volunteering as an interpretive guide for the Dick Proenneke Site at Twin Lakes.